Love

Good Luck & Best Wishes

Dave Herbeck

An Act of
Love

Preparing Your Spouse
for Life Without You
a financial guide

DAVID J. HERBECK
CPA/PFS, ChFC

Beaver's Pond Press, Inc.
Edina, Minnesota

This book is intended to provide general information. The publisher and author cannot assume responsibility for individual decisions made by readers. Should assistance be required for the type of advice and services discussed in this book, professionals should be consulted. References to tax provisions in this book are based on current laws and regulations. Annual revisions in the tax law, when and if adopted, could change planning done under current law.

ISBN 1-59298-078-3

Library of Congress Catalog Number: 2004110658

Printed in the United States of America

First Printing: August 2004

08 07 06 05 04   5 4 3 2 1

Beaver's Pond Press, Inc.

7104 Ohms Lane, Suite 216
Edina, MN 55439
(952) 829-8818
www.beaverspondpress.com

to order, visit *www.BookHouseFulfillment.com*
or call 1-800-901-3480. Reseller discounts available.

David Herbeck (763 546-6211) is a registered representative of, and securities are offered through, HD Vest Investment Services[SM,] Member: SIPC, Advisory services are offered through H.D. Vest Advisory Services[SM,] non-bank subsidiaries of Wells Fargo & Company, 6333 North State Highway 161, Fourth Floor, Irving, Texas 75038, (972) 870-6000.

To my mother Violet who has been widowed twice and always has shown character and strength

To my loving wife Deb and my two children; Ashley and Brittany for being patient and putting up with me while I dedicated my time to this book

To all of my clients for allowing me to serve them and gain insight for this book

Contents

*P*art *T*wo
Ready or Not
Activities Needed Within Nine Months of Death

Contents

$\mathscr{P}$*art* $\mathscr{T}$*hree*
A New Life

Acknowledgments

I would like to thank the following people for their expertise and time:

Dave Bolfik, CLU, ChFC—Life, Disability and Long-Term Care insurance review

William W. McReavy—Funeral Preplanning guidance and review

John Olmon, Attorney-at-Law—Estate Planning review

Debra Herbeck—Computer assistance

Wendy Nemitz—Marketing support

Thanks to my partners at
Blanski Peter Kronlage & Zoch P.A.
for their patience and understanding:

John Csargo, CPA, MBT, CFP®

John Edson, CPA, CMA, CVA

Phil Kronlage, CPA

David Thorp, CPA

Gary Turnquist, CPA

Jim Wehmhoff, CPA

Introduction

Losing a spouse is one of the most difficult challenges a human being is ever likely to face. No matter if you are married 2 years or 40 years, such a significant loss is hard to accept. All of your future plans and dreams are suddenly changed or erased. And, difficult as it may seem, you must carry on. Fortunately, in most cases, family members and friends will be there to support you. In addition, numerous community or church support groups are available to offer assistance. The important thing is that you find whatever it takes to help you move forward.

My mother was widowed twice, once when I was 15 years old and again in 2002, when I was 46. She has handled these situations as well as anyone I have ever seen. When she needed financial or legal advice she sought out professionals who could help her. She knew these were not her areas of expertise. (I believe this is wise, because people who try to do these things themselves are more apt to make errors, and in many situations errors may cost more than if they had just paid for a professional's help.) Mom also realized early on that she needed to stay socially active and keep busy. Now a weekend seldom passes that she is not out at the local ballroom having a good time with her large circle of friends. Most weekdays she also has activities planned.

Her strength just shines through in so many ways. She definitely has found the key to a longer life!

I have never lost a spouse, yet I deal with widows all the time. As a financial advisor and CPA, my clientele includes a large number of widows, and I pride myself on the work I do assisting them. In some situations, after the loss of a spouse, I am the first professional they see. Other times they are introduced to me at a later date. Either way, I specialize in assisting them with all of their financial tasks—the subject of this book. Married people work with me, as well, to ensure their spouse will be taken care of after they are gone. Even if they have handled their finances themselves over the years, at a certain point in life most people want the peace of mind of knowing their spouse will have someone to rely on after they are gone.

This book was written for both men and women. However, statistically it is more likely to be used by women. The Women's Life Insurance Society performed a study in 2003 and found the average age of widowhood for women to be 56. Another statistic from the Social Security Administration in 2003 shows why more women are widows—on average they live five to ten years longer than men do!

Does the following scenario sound familiar to you? One spouse handles the finances in the family and always has. They handle all the financial issues in the household, such as paying bills, dealing with life, health, and property insurance, and managing investments. This person generally understands the family's investments and believes they are in control. They may be a do-it-yourself-type person who can handle things on their own. Or they may understand things but use a broker to make suggestions and complete transactions for them. Either way, investments are not discussed between spouses, because it is not seen as a problem.

This is not an unusual situation in many households. Most of us feel invincible and do not think we are going to die. As a result we may feel no urgency to make sure our surviving spouse will be taken care of. But we do know that the older we get the greater the chance of something happening.

I wrote this book to assist you in three ways:

1. To help you prepare for widowhood, while your spouse is still alive;

2. To give you a step-by-step guide on what to do in the first nine months after your loved one's death; and

3. To help you, living as a widow, properly plan for your financial future.

Whether you receive this book before you are widowed or after, I hope it will give you the guidance to deal with this difficult situation and take some of the stress out of it. To simplify, I will use the term "widow," but it applies to either gender. This book does not focus on grief issues; I am not qualified to address them and leave it to the professionals who specialize in grief counseling. I believe everything will get better sooner if you can keep a positive attitude and keep humor in your life. Throughout the book, I have included some of my favorite jokes for your enjoyment.

I chose to call the book *An Act of Love* because that is truly how I see this type of planning. I have encountered too many situations that were much more difficult than they should have been because people failed to plan, either knowingly or unknowingly. After reading this book, if you still fail to plan, it would be most unfortunate. So, do what is right for your spouse, and commit "An Act of Love."

Part One

Preparing for Widowhood

Before everything else,
getting ready is the secret of success.
—Henry Ford

There are some things in life that you can prepare for. Some are important and others are meaningless in the big picture. If you love your spouse, you can give them no greater gift than having your affairs arranged so it will be easier for them to carry on after you are gone. Losing a spouse is hard enough without getting tied up in a confusing legal and financial jungle for which you are unprepared. After doing a lot of research on this issue, I could not find one book that addressed it. This book will give you some useful suggestions on how to prepare in a way that can make the passing of your spouse just a little bit more bearable.

Whenever you start a task, it's best to start at the beginning. The first step in making your financial life easier is to set up a good record keeping system. The following chapter will give you a framework for getting organized.

Record Keeping

One of the easiest things you can do to simplify your life is to set up a good filing system. Nothing is more frustrating than trying to find a document you know you have but just can't find. You and your spouse may already have such a system, and that's great, but if you don't, now is the time to set one up.

The first step is to identify a place where you can work. You may have an office in your house or you may be able to set up shop in a spare bedroom. This workspace is where you should work on your finances. Having a separate space will make it less likely for you to mix important financial papers with everyday items and misplace them. Ideally, you will have a desk to work on. If not, a table will do.

You will also need to buy a filing cabinet if you don't have one or have space in the one you have. If you purchase a new one, I would suggest at least a two-drawer file. Next, purchase two dozen expandable hanging file folders. Each one of these will be labeled with one of the bold titles in the following list, such as Banking or Investments. Lastly, purchase at least four dozen 8½" x 11" manila filing folders.

These manila folders should be titled with the sub-headings that follow, such as Checking or Cancelled Checks. Place them in the hanging file folders titled with the appropriate bold heading. If you need more room, create a second hanging file with the same title.

Listed below are the categories along with the documents you will file in each.

Banking

- Checking Account Statements
- Cancelled Checks (if your bank returns them to you)
- Check Registers (for old registers)
- Savings Account Statements

Investments

- Brokerage Statements
- Mutual Fund Statements
- Money Market Statements
- Stock and Bond Certificates
- U.S. Bonds, Notes/T-Bills
- IRA Statements
- 401(k) Statements
- Annuity Statements
- Certificates of Deposit
- Contracts for Deed

Insurance

- Life Insurance
- Health Insurance
- Long-Term Care Insurance
- Homeowner Insurance
- Auto Insurance
- Disability Insurance

Personal Documents

- Birth Certificates
- Death Certificates
- Marriage Certificates
- Passports
- Social Security (cards and statements)
- Military (discharge papers)
- Safety Deposit Box (information and key)
- Divorce
- Safe Combination

Tax Returns

- Current and Prior Years Income Tax Returns
- Estimated Tax Coupons
- Current Year Tax Related Documents (W-2s, 1099s, charitable information, etc.)
- Other Tax Returns (such as trust tax returns, etc.)

Estate Planning Documents

- Wills
- Living Trust
- Advanced Directive (Living Will or Health Care Directive)
- Powers of Attorney
- Burial Instructions
- Prenuptial or Postnuptial Agreements
- Preplanned Funeral Arrangements

Employer information

- Stock Option Programs
- Paycheck Stubs
- COBRA (Health insurance continuation paperwork)
- Deferred Compensation

Household

- House Purchase Settlement Papers
- Mortgage Document
- Refinance Papers
- Real Estate Taxes
- Appraisals
- Major Improvements (receipts)

- Deed (if house has no mortgage)

Warranties

- Homeowners
- Auto
- Furniture
- Appliances
- Electronics
- Miscellaneous

Automobiles:

- Titles
- Repair Receipts
- License
- Registration

Businesses

- Stock Certificates
- Buy-Sell Agreements
- Partnership Agreements

Debts

- Loan Payments (Home, Auto, College, etc.)
- Automatic Payments
- Credit Card Statements (or, you may want to create a file per credit card, labeled "Visa," "Discover," etc.)

Current Bills

- Set up a manila folder for each type of bill you are paying such as insurance, utilities, telephone, etc. Include a miscellaneous compartment for those one-time nonrecurring bills.

After you pay your current bills as detailed in the Bill Paying section of Chapter 25, "Financial Issues," in Part III, file your receipts in the appropriately titled manila folder. By doing this you will be able to locate quickly and easily any bill you paid. At the end of the year, empty each folder of paid bills into separate envelopes and label them. Put all of the envelopes into a box or bigger envelope and write the year on the outside of it. In the future, if you ever need to find a receipt from a previous year, all you have to do is find the box or envelope for the correct year and look in the appropriate envelope.

If you are concerned about security issues that may arise from storing items like a safe deposit box key in a file, consider purchasing a file cabinet that is protected with a lock and key.

If you take the time to organize your information in this manner, you will have less stress going forward when you need to find your records.

Financial Awareness

The most difficult situations I encounter are when a spouse passes away and the surviving spouse does not know what they own or where it is located. It is then necessary to spend time going through all of the paperwork and statements the surviving spouse can find and verify what is owned and which accounts are still active. There are times that an account will turn up a year after death. In one situation, one of my partners discovered a client had many shares of stock held by a transfer agent that no one knew about. The value of the stock in that account was over $2,000,000. It seems hard to believe, but if both spouses do not have an understanding of the investment holdings, it can happen.

Thus, it is extremely important for both spouses to be aware of the family's financial situation. I am not suggesting that you need to be an investment professional, but each spouse should have a general understanding of the types of investments you own and why you own them. In addition, you will need to know where your accounts are set up and the name and number of your investment advisor or advisors. In Part I, Chapter 4, "Estate Planning for Married

Couples," I will give you an organizational tool that you can use to record where all your accounts are held.

You can do several things to become more educated on financial matters. For instance, if one spouse has not been responsible for a checking account, this spouse will need to become familiar with operating a checking account. One way to do this is to have both spouses open their own checking accounts. At the end of the month, you can work together to balance the accounts. One of the checkbooks could be used sparingly; the reason to have it is to become more familiar with the process. If you do not like the idea of opening a second checking account, you can take turns being responsible for the family's main checking account.

To gain more knowledge about the workings of the investment world, the financially inexperienced spouse could open up an investment or IRA account. This would help breed familiarity with investment statements and brokerage accounts. And this spouse may want to take a class in managing money. Your local community college may offer this type of program. Whatever you do, the time you invest in becoming better educated and more financially aware will be well worth it down the road.

Establishing Credit

A good credit record is very valuable to a widow. It will be one less issue to deal with when a spouse passes away. It will be to your advantage to do this while both spouses are alive. As the potentially surviving spouse, you may not need any credit in your own name right now, but I will guarantee you now is the time you should be establishing your own credit record. There are a couple of reasons for this.

First, and a fact which may surprise you, if you go to a bank when you really need credit, it is much harder to get. The best time to establish credit is when you do not need it. Usually when everything is fine financially the bank will gladly extend you credit. Unfortunately, when things turn bad and you need help you often cannot get it. So, I urge you to obtain credit in your name while it is easy to get.

Second, if you have no credit record, even if not in need, credit is much harder to get. I just helped a client obtain a mortgage. She was 82 years old and always paid her bills. Her only problem was that she never had established any loans in her name to produce a history of making timely payments. Because she had no credit record, the bank made her provide an enormous amount of proof that she paid her bills before they would lend her the money. The whole process would have been a lot easier had she borrowed money at some time and established a record of paying the money back. One way to do this is to get a credit card in your name and pay the balance in full each month. The charges do not need to be large, just enough to document that you are a responsible person and pay your bills on time.

Emergency Funds

Another thing I've learned from my experience working with the recently widowed is how important it is to have access to money. If you are ever in an emergency and need money right now, do you know how you are going to get it? Many people do not. When one spouse dies, bank accounts and other assets may be tied up in the probate process and adequate funds may not be available for the surviving spouse. This is a real emergency and can force the surviving spouse or a caring relative to sell an asset, such as a stock or bond, to obtain cash. The value of the asset sold may be depressed at the time of sale, and that compounds the problem.

Most experts advise keeping on hand three to six months of living expenses in case of emergency. And by "on hand" I do not mean keeping cash at home! I once knew a gentleman who grew up during the Depression. His parents had lost all the money they had, which was in a bank at that time. Because of this experience, he never trusted banks and instead kept his cash around the house. When he passed away, cash was found hidden in books, magazines, cabinets, and every other place you could imagine. And it certainly wasn't earning any interest!

Three to six months of living expenses can be quite a sum, but if you set this much aside you'll feel and be much more secure. Another option is to have a line of credit available to obtain funds in an emergency. Most banks will let you set up a nonsecured line of credit or a home equity line secured by your house. This does not cost a lot to set up, and it can give you access to funds in an emergency. The amount you borrow can be repaid when your situation improves. The advantage of a home equity line of credit is that you are able to deduct the interest paid on your tax return. The disadvantage is that if the loan is not repaid you are putting your house at risk. If it is not advantageous to itemize your deductions, a nonsecured line of credit is preferred since there will be no tax benefit. If you are unsure as to whether you will have the means to repay the loan, use a nonsecured line of credit to avoid putting your home at risk for defaulting on the loan.

Chapter Three

Choosing a Financial Services Professional

You may be the type of individual who is experienced and knowledgeable in managing your family's investments. But if something happens to you, your spouse will be left with an account containing investments they do not understand. It is essential for you and your spouse to choose a financial advisor with whom you are both comfortable. This will be the person your spouse will work with after you are gone or unable to continue handling these tasks. Selecting a financial service professional can be a challenge. Let me share a joke with you that might bring home the point…

One day, John Doe passed away and found himself standing at the pearly gates. There he encountered St. Peter, who explained the rules to him. He had a choice of whether he wanted to go to heaven or hell. First, St. Peter told him he needed to spend a day in hell, so he was put on an elevator for the long ride down. When the doors opened John was expecting fire and a horny-tailed devil, but instead a gentleman in a suit greeted him. The politely mannered gentlemen gave him a tour. John could not believe his eyes. On his left was a beau-

tiful golf course, and on his right was a wonderful beach with people lying in the sun. As they walked, they passed nice restaurants, theaters, and concert halls. Well, John was certainly impressed. At the end of the day, he got back on the elevator and returned to St. Peter. St. Peter told John to get a good night's rest because the next day he would visit heaven.

The next day came and John went to heaven. There he found a nice, relaxing scene where people were lying about on billowy clouds, with nice music playing in the background. All of the people seemed very happy, content and at peace with themselves. After the day was over John returned to St. Peter where he was told he would have a night to think it over.

The next morning came and it was time for John's decision. St. Peter asked him what his decision was. John said he was embarrassed, but he had to choose hell. Heaven was nice but he liked the more active life he had witnessed in hell. St. Peter said he would grant John his wish and put him back on the elevator for his ride down to hell.

When the doors opened, John was shocked. He saw fire, people performing hard labor, and a little horny-tailed devil. John asked the devil what happened to the golf course, beach, restaurants, and entertainment areas. The devil replied, "John, yesterday you were a prospect and today you are a client."

Do not let this happen to you when picking an advisor.

The type of individual you need is someone who is a well-rounded financial services professional. Well-rounded means this person will have received training and be experienced in the following areas:

- Income Taxes
- Investments
- Insurance
- Estate Planning
- Retirement Planning
- Cash-Flow Planning

Each area makes up an important part of financial planning. To prepare a comprehensive financial plan each of these components should be addressed.

Many professional designations require that an individual show proficiency in each of these areas to earn the right to use that designation. Next are three common designations that prepare advisors to work with people on a comprehensive basis.

Professional Designations

ChFC (Chartered Financial Consultant)—This designation is obtained through the American College in Bryn Mawr, Pennsylvania. For 76 years, the American College has provided quality self-study courses for financial services professionals. The ChFC program provides financial advisors, and others in the financial services industry, with in-depth knowledge of the skills needed to perform comprehensive financial planning for their clients. The designation requires eight courses: five required and three electives. Students also must complete a minimum amount of ongoing education, as well as specified experience requirements, maintain ethical standards, and agree to comply with the American College's code of ethics.

CFP (Certified Financial Planner)—The CFP program is for professionals seeking the knowledge and skills necessary to objectively assess a client's current financial status, identify problem areas, and recommend appropriate actions; in essence, to provide comprehensive, client-based financial planning. The designation requires knowledge of estate planning, tax preparation, retirement planning, insurance, and investing. The successful completion of a two-day, 10-hour comprehensive test is required. Students also must complete a minimum amount of ongoing education as well as specified experience requirements, maintain ethical standards, and agree to comply with the Certified Financial Planners Board's code of ethics and professional responsibility.

PFS (Personal Financial Specialist)—To qualify for the PFS designation offered by the American Institute of Certified Public Accountants (AICPA), an applicant must:

1. Be a member in good standing of the AICPA;

2. Hold a valid and unrevoked CPA certificate issued by a legally constituted state authority;

3. Have at least 250 hours of experience per year in personal financial planning activities for the three years immediately preceding the application. This experience must include the personal financial planning process, personal income tax planning, risk management planning, investment planning, retirement planning, and estate planning;

4. Agree to comply with all the requirements for reaccredidation;

5. Pass the PFS examination; and

6. Upon successful completion of the PFS exam, six references must be submitted to substantiate working experience in personal financial planning.

While choosing a planner who has one or more of the above designations does not guarantee they will be the best financial planner in the world, it does show that they have spent time and effort to secure education and experience and to enhance their skills in the area of financial planning.

Questions to Ask a Financial Services Professional

1. What experience do you have in working with people in my situation?

Why would you ask the question in this manner? I believe it is not enough to just choose an advisor with experience. The experience should match your situation. If you are retired or a widow, find someone who works with retired people or widows, not someone who assists younger people in accumulating funds for retirement. The odds are they will be more familiar with the issues you will be facing and better able to serve you.

2. **What credentials do you have?**

   Remember to look for the designations mentioned previously: the ChFC, CFP, or the PFS.

3. **What value can you add for me that another planner can't?**

   I believe it is best to work with someone who can look at your whole picture and assist you. An advisor with a tax background can add a lot of value. When you make an investment decision, generally there is a tax ramification somewhere in the future. Your advisor needs to understand this. In addition, cash-flow planning requires a strong tax background. It is not just a matter of which account to withdraw funds from, but how the withdrawal can be done in the most tax-efficient manner. In addition, knowledge of estate taxation can also add value for you. Coordinating your investment planning with tax planning can save you and your heirs many dollars. An individual with an insurance license or insurance knowledge can also help give you guidance in those areas.

4. **How do you charge for your services?**

It is important to know how financial service professionals charge for their work. The two most common methods are *fees*, in the form of asset management charges, and *commissions*, based on financial transactions. Some advisors charge fees and some charge commissions. Some may charge both ways, depending on how the client would like to pay.

Fees. If you use an asset management account, you will be charged a percent of the assets you are having managed. This fee is generally determined by the size of your account, and is normally in the 1–2% range. Under this type of arrangement, you are not charged a commission when investments are purchased or sold for you. If your account balance goes up over time, your fee also goes up. If your account balance decreases, so does your fee. Some people believe this type of arrangement is the best because it takes away the doubt as to whether a transaction is made for the benefit of you or the planner. The services that you receive for the management fee will vary from advisor to advisor. Make sure to ask what you are getting for the fee you are paying. The fees are not comparable unless the same services are offered.

Commissions. Under this compensation model, the planner is paid each time a transaction (buy or sell) takes place, including the purchase or sale of items such as stocks and bonds. In addition, a planner is paid a commission when you purchase an interest in a mutual fund. There are many types of financial products available. Ask your planner how they will be compensated before the transaction is completed.

5. **Have you ever been suspended or disciplined?**

   This question can help uncover any potential problems. Find out what organizations the advisor is regulated by and check their background. The American College, Certified Financial Planning Board, and the American Institute of Certified Public Accountants regulate the designations identified earlier. In addition, you can check with the NASD (National Association of Securities Dealers) to find out if the planner or the firm they work for has any record of complaints against them.

6. **Who will be in charge of my account?**

   If you are comfortable with the person you are interviewing, make sure that this person will be working with you. In addition, ask to meet the advisor's assistant, because this person generally will be assisting you with account and paperwork issues in the future. You might also want to find out how long the person has been working with their broker/dealer. A broker/dealer is any individual or firm in the business of buying and selling securities for themselves and others. Broker/dealers must register with the Securities Exchange Commission. Some advisors have a habit of moving around. This is not good for you because if the advisor moves again your choice will be to work with someone new, who you don't know, or to follow the advisor to a new broker/dealer, which results in all new paperwork having to be completed for your accounts. My recommendation is to work with someone who displays stability.

7. **How often will we meet?**

   I believe financial advisors should meet at least quarterly with their clients. The last thing you want is to set up an account and never hear from your advisor, or simply to have perfunctory annual meetings.

8. **Do you require a minimum amount of investments to manage?**

   Before you spend too much time with someone, make sure you qualify for their services. Some advisors will require that you invest a minimum amount with them (such as $300,000 or more) before they will accept you as a client.

9. **Would you give me some references?**

It is a good idea to speak with some of the advisor's current clients to see if they are happy and comfortable with them.

10. **What professional organizations do you belong to?**

Belonging to professional organizations can show the person is committed to their profession and working to improve it.

Whether you are looking for an advisor to assist you now or would just like to find one to assist you or your spouse at a later date, this is a worthwhile endeavor. Even if you are in good health now, do not let this stop you from doing your homework of finding a qualified person to serve as your financial advisor. You never know when you or your spouse will need someone to step in and help. If you follow the guidelines just listed, and are successful in your search, you will have one less thing to worry about when the time of need arrives.

Chapter Four

Estate Planning for Married Couples

"Estate planning" is a broad term that entails many possible planning issues. The ultimate goal of good estate planning is to ensure that the intended people inherit your property in the simplest manner, while minimizing estate taxes. In this chapter, I am going to focus on planning as it relates to a married couple. Planning for singles will be covered in Chapter 30, "Estate Planning for Singles," in Part III.

The goal is to allow a couple to prepare their estate in such a way as to make it as simple as possible when one spouse passes away, while minimizing the amount of estate tax the surviving spouse must pay. The federal government allows an individual to pass a maximum specified amount onto their heirs without having to pay an estate tax. The allowance is known as the applicable exclusion amount (see Table 1). To take advantage of this exclusion, your estate must be structured correctly.

Realizing that many complicated situations, such as business ownership, are beyond the scope of this book,

Table 1. Applicable Exclusion Amount

Year	Amount
✦ 2004	$1,500,000
✦ 2005	$1,500,000
✦ 2006	$2,000,000
✦ 2007	$2,000,000
✦ 2008	$2,000,000
✦ 2009	$3,500,000
✦ 2010	Repealed
✦ 2011	$1,000,000

the following discussion focuses on a typical estate where the assets consist of retirement plans, normal investment accounts, and residential real estate. The example also assumes that the couple lives in a state that is *not* a community property state. Community property states are Arizona, California, Idaho, Louisiana, Nevada, New Mexico, Texas, Washington, and Wisconsin. If you live in one of these states, some adjustments will need to be made to the documents depicted in this chapter.

Another issue that has arisen over the last few years is that a number of states have not adopted recent changes made to the estate tax law at the federal level. Previously these states tied their state estate tax to the federal rules, and computed the tax based on the taxable estate derived on the federal estate tax return. Now, however, the states have adopted their own rules and levels of exemption. This makes estate planning more complicated. Because many states have different rules, they will not be discussed individually here, but you should become informed of any differences in your state.

When a spouse passes away life feels difficult enough without having to worry about dealing with probate or other complicated estate planning issues. Preparing ahead of time will make things a bit easier. The disability of a spouse during a long illness or prior to death may also be anticipated and addressed with proper planning.

The planning documents covered in this section are Wills, Revocable Living Trusts, Durable Powers of Attorney and Advance Directives (also known as Living Wills or Health Care Directives). Your situation will dictate which documents are right for you. Generally, when you have a trust or will drafted, the attorney will prepare a durable power of attorney and an advance directive at the same time. *Do not* try to draft these documents on your own. An accomplished estate planning attorney should be used to draft all legal documents for you.

You may already have an attorney you work with. If not, the attorney you select should have experience in drafting estate planning documents. Numerous sources exist to assist you with your search. The best way to find an attorney is by obtaining a referral. If you need an attorney, ask your family or friends which attorney they use or have used and if they were satisfied. You may also contact the State Bar Association. They should have a referral service for practicing attorneys in your area. Another possibility is to contact the National Academy of Elder Law Attorneys. Use their Web site to search for an attorney (www.naela.com.) You can also reach them by telephone at (520) 881-4005. If you decide to use the yellow pages, and do not have a personal referral, make sure you interview more than one potential attorney.

Using the proper legal documents and having your assets titled properly makes it possible to minimize what needs to be done after death. This does not, however, mean that no further legal work will be required. But you will have done what you can to help the process along.

Attorneys are very important to putting an estate plan in place, and I work closely with many of them. However, I can't help myself and have to share an attorney joke . . .

There was this fellow who was on vacation in San Francisco, and he had to return home the next day. He was in Chinatown and wanted to bring home a memento of his trip, so he stopped in a gift shop. While browsing, he saw a bronzed rat. For some reason, he was fascinated with it and wanted it for a souvenir. He *took it up to the counter and asked the clerk how much it cost. The clerk said that it depended on whether he wanted to purchase the story behind the bronzed rat, or just the rat itself. The price for the story was $100 and the rat was $10. The fellow said he didn't need to know the story, but he would take the rat. He handed the clerk $10 and left the store with his bronzed rat.*

Soon, walking down the street, he heard small footsteps behind him. He turned around and noticed a couple of rats were following him. This made him nervous, so he walked a little faster. He heard more footsteps and turned around to find 50 rats following him. He began to run slowly, and he could hear the footsteps getting louder. This time when he turned around there was a whole city block full of rats following him. Now he panicked and began to run as fast as he could. He ran all the way to San Francisco Bay. When he reached the bay he raised the bronzed rat up into the air and hurled it into the bay. To his amazement, all of the rats followed it into the water and drowned. He could not believe it. He decided he had to go back to the gift store.

When he walked in, the clerk of the store was standing at the counter with a big smile on his face. He asked, "Now do you want to know the story behind the bronzed rat?" The fellow said, "No, but I would like to know if you have any bronzed attorneys."

Wills

Many adults I encounter do not have a will or any kind of estate planning documents. I find this alarming, but not unbelievable. Many people do not want to deal with their own mortality, and others do not worry about it because any problems that will result will happen when they are gone. This leads to the question, "Is this what you want for your spouse?"

What is a will? A will is a legal instrument that documents how you want your estate to be distributed and who you would like to oversee the process. Everyone should have a will, whether it is for estate tax planning, for ensuring that your assets go where you would like, or to appoint guardians for minor children.

The major questions that are answered by a will are:

* Who will inherit your assets?

* When will they inherit your assets?

* Who will be your personal representative and supervise the process?

* Who will be the guardian of your minor children (if you have them)?

* Are there any specific requests you would like carried out?

As you can see, there are many reasons to have a will. One important thing to remember: *A will does not control assets that have a beneficiary designation or assets that pass to another person by law.* For example, retirement accounts that include IRAs have beneficiaries and are not controlled by a will. The same applies to life insurance proceeds. If your bank accounts or brokerage accounts utilize "pay on death" or "transfer on death" clauses, they also would not be affected. Similarly, assets owned jointly with right of survivorship pass by law and are not controlled by a will.

Many types of wills exist. The following describes the types of wills to which you are most likely to be introduced.

Simple Wills. This is the most basic type of will. In the simplest terms, it states that if one spouse dies before the other all assets will pass to the surviving spouse. The simple will also contains a provision for what will happen to your estate if both spouses pass away simultaneously. Usually it will dictate the use of a trust if you have minor children or concerns about the financial responsibility of one of the secondary beneficiaries named in your will. Their share of the estate will be held in trust for their benefit. The trust would generally be dissolved when the children reach a predetermined age after adulthood has been reached. If the provision is for an adult who is not properly equipped to handle finances, the trust may last for their lifetime. A simple will is commonly used for estates that have a value less than the amount allowed to be passed tax free by law, known as the applicable exclusion amount (see Table 1). It may be used if you don't expect your estate to grow larger than this amount in the future. Estate, in this case, means the total value of all assets owned by both spouses. If your estate is less than the applicable exclusion amount, you may skip ahead a couple of pages to the section titled "Living Trusts."

Disclaimer Wills. A disclaimer will provides much more flexibility than a simple will. It can act the same as a simple will, but if there is a need to avoid estate taxes, it can also be a good vehicle for this purpose. A disclaimer will leaves everything to the beneficiaries named, just as a simple will does. However, if the estate is large enough to be subject to estate tax, more planning opportunities are available. Here is an example of how a disclaimer will works.

> *John Doe dies in 2004 and has a disclaimer will in place. John's will dictates that all assets go to his wife, Jane, who is the sole beneficiary of John's estate. If John's estate is large enough to be subject to the estate tax, Jane can disclaim some or all of the assets from the estate—in other words, not accept the assets. The law permits John's estate to pass on $1,500,000 (the applicable exclusion amount in 2004) without paying any tax in 2004. So, if John's estate totaled $4,000,000, Jane could accept $2,500,000 of John's assets from the estate and disclaim the other $1,500,000. The $1,500,000 would then go to the disclaimer trust, which would be the secondary beneficiary, named in the will. Jane would then be able to receive the income from the*

trust and could obtain the principal, with the trustee's discretion, for health, education, support, and maintenance expenses to the level of her accustomed manner of living. The principal remaining in the trust at Jane's death passes to the beneficiaries of the trust, generally the couple's children. By doing this, the disclaimer will has protected $1,500,000 (John's applicable exclusion amount) from estate tax. Had Jane not utilized the disclaimer provision in the will, John's applicable exclusion amount would have been wasted.

When using a disclaimer will your assets will need to be titled properly. In most cases, if possible, try to have an equal amount of assets in each spouse's name. This may be difficult due to a number of possible problems. Sometimes all of the assets are in one spouse's name in the form of a retirement plan. You may need to designate your residence to one spouse in order to give each spouse assets to own. Your attorney should advise you about this when you implement these wills.

If you and your spouse have disclaimer wills and one spouse passes away, it is essential that the surviving spouse meet with your attorney before withdrawing or using any of the money that could be disclaimed. The disclaimer must be made within nine months of death, and it is important that all of the rules are followed. *I cannot stress enough that when you are dealing with these types of issues, consult a professional and do not try to do it yourself.*

If your estate is greater than the applicable exclusion amount, a disclaimer will could be the appropriate choice for your estate planning vehicle. A disclaimer will may also be a useful estate planning tool for much larger estates.

Because of the uncertainty of the current estate tax law and the changing amounts that may be left tax free (see Table 1), a disclaimer will can be quite efficient at handling a variety of situations. Disclaimer planning postpones the decision of how much, if anything, will pass to the surviving spouse. It allows us to delay answering this question until we know the amount and character of the assets, needs of the surviving spouse, and what the tax law is at the date of death. Planning is a bit more difficult in today's environment, but hopefully the law will be fixed soon so that some future certainty is restored.

AB Trust Will (also known as Credit Trust Will or Bypass Trust Will)—This type of instrument has been the most common estate planning tool for individuals who have estates large enough to be subject to estate taxes. It requires an amount equal to the applicable exclusion amount to be set aside in a trust known as a credit trust. The surviving spouse would then be able to receive the income from the trust and could obtain the principal, with the trustee's discretion, for health, education, support, and maintenance expenses to the level of their accustomed manner of living. The principal remaining in the trust at the surviving spouse's death passes to the beneficiaries of the trust, generally the couple's children. As with the disclaimer will, asset titling is a key ingredient in making this type of will successful. Each spouse must have assets titled in their own name.

The AB trust will is still an applicable estate planning vehicle, but with the annual exclusion amount going up I believe it is better used for estates that are at least double the size of the applicable exclusion amount. This is hard to do, since the amount of exclusion will increase from 2006–2009 and then decrease in 2010 and 2011. Eventually, I think Congress will fix the exclusion at some amount closer to the $3,500,000 that will be allowed in 2009. Obviously I can't assure you of this, but you do have to use some assumptions when planning.

Because of the uncertainty regarding the changing applicable exclusion amount, I would only use this type of will if your estate is over $7,000,000. If your estate is less than this amount but more than the applicable exclusion amount, I believe the disclaimer will would be the best choice. In the past, many estates have been set up utilizing an AB trust will that would put all assets into the credit trust to the extent estate taxes could be avoided. Estates that have an AB trust will in place today could cause a problem. Repeal of the estate tax would be a disaster for people with AB trust wills because the credit trust would end up with all of the assets controlled by the AB trust will and the surviving spouse may end up with nothing. See the example at the end of this chapter in the section titled "Review Periodically."

Living Trusts

The previous section covered wills as estate planning documents, but if you were to look in your local paper and see the seminar ads you would think a living trust is the only estate planning tool you should use. And, actually, a living trust can be a very appropriate estate planning tool. However, it is not the only tool and not always the best depending on the situation. A living trust is a private document, where a will is a public document. After a person passes away, their will is available to anybody who wants to go to the probate court and view the will. Assets owned by a living trust are not subject to probate. Probate can be expensive and time consuming. (For a more in-depth discussion of Probate, see Chapter 16 in Part II.)

A living trust can be used in the same manner as the wills mentioned above: the simple, disclaimer, and AB trusts. The plans basically work the same as those mentioned previously, but participants receive added benefits provided by a living trust such as privacy and probate avoidance.

A pour-over will must be used in conjunction with a living trust. The pour-over will states that if you owned any assets at death that were not owned in the name of the trust, they should now be put into the trust. This is necessary because if all of your assets are not titled in the name of the trust when you pass away, there has to be a way to get those assets into your trust.

When is a living trust the better estate planning vehicle? The following paragraphs summarize several points for you to consider.

Privacy. As mentioned earlier, it is very important to some people to keep their affairs private, and a living trust does just that. In most situations, I do not believe anyone cares what you have or would go to the county offices to look at your will. However, this degree of privacy is important to some people and this is a decision individuals must make for themselves.

Probate. This is a major reason people use living trusts. Obviously, if the probate process can be avoided it would be a good thing. You will generally incur legal fees when going through the probate process because *this is not a task you should attempt to perform without the guidance of an attorney.* Probate also delays wrapping up the estate and may even inhibit the surviving spouse's ability to get at the estate's assets for a period of time. Avoiding probate can also be important if you own real estate in more than one state. In this situation you could be subject to probate in two or more different states. As you can see, there are many reasons to avoid probate. Some people simply acknowledge, "We do not want to leave a mess for our children."

Asset Management. You may be in a situation where you are concerned that you may become mentally or physically incompetent and will not be able to manage your assets. And your spouse may not have the necessary expertise to do so. By setting up a living trust you are designating a trustee to take over those duties when you are no longer able to handle them.

When might you consider using a will instead of a living trust?

Small estate. A small estate with no real estate or where beneficiary designations can be used to avoid probate can get by without a living trust. (See the following section, "Avoiding Probate.")

Large age difference between spouses. If a large age difference exists between spouses you may not want to use a living trust. If the surviving spouse is young the assets will be tied up in that trust for a very long time.

You do not follow through. If you choose to use a living trust you will need to retitle your assets in the name of the trust. When you purchase new assets, you will need to purchase them in the name of the trust. If you do not do this, and leave assets titled incorrectly, you could still be subject to probate, which would defeat the purpose of having the living trust. Any assets titled incorrectly would end up in the trust because of the pour-over will discussed previously, but they would not avoid probate.

Probate does not concern you. Many people are not concerned about probate and do not want to incur the additional costs involved in setting up a living trust.

Many positives and negatives can be determined for

using a trust versus a will. You will need to meet with an attorney to determine what is right for you. A living trust costs more to set up but saves money when you pass away, as there should be no probate and wrapping up the estate is simpler. The type of vehicle you ultimately use is your decision.

Avoiding Probate

Is there a way to avoid probate without using a living trust? There sure is! Titling your assets correctly can do it.

Any assets that are controlled by your will are subject to probate. The idea is to title assets so that they pass automatically—using joint tenancy or a beneficiary designation so they will not be controlled by your will. People whose estate is less than the applicable exclusion amount (listed in Table 1) can use this strategy. Larger estates will need to title their assets in a fashion that works best with the estate planning documents they have put in place.

If an asset is owned in any of the following forms, probate will be avoided because the asset passes directly, by law or beneficiary designation, and will not be controlled by your will.

Joint Tenancy with right of survivorship. When you pass away, your spouse (the joint tenant) becomes 100% owner of any asset titled in this manner. This is common for real estate, such as the family home.

IRA beneficiary designation. Unless your estate is listed as the beneficiary (which it should not be) it should not be subject to probate.

Payable on Death (POD). Any bank savings, checking, or money market account offers this feature, which will avoid probate on these assets.

Transfer on Death (TOD). This stipulation can be applied to your brokerage or investment accounts to avoid probate.

All of the above methods will work for married couples. However, if you are married, the most effective way to make this work is to use beneficiary designations such as payable on death or transfer on death for all of your accounts except real estate. The real estate would have to be owned jointly. After the first spouse's death, the surviving spouse will own all of the assets.

This strategy is not foolproof. Keep in mind that if both spouses die at the same time, the spouse considered to die last will have their estate subject to probate. The only asset in their estate that may be subject to probate is the real estate, because all of the other accounts with beneficiary designations could have secondary beneficiaries. Nonetheless, the real estate would still be subject to probate, causing the estate to go through the probate process. Even if only one spouse passes away, more planning will have to be done after the first death to ensure that the second estate will not be subject to probate (discussed in Part III). In light of this, if you do not have a living trust, it is still wise to take the steps mentioned here to greatly minimize the chances of being subject to probate on the first death.

Durable Power of Attorney

The durable power of attorney is an essential document for your estate plan. This is a short document, inexpensive to have drafted, but very important. It allows you to name an agent to manage your financial affairs if you become incapacitated. Generally, you would name your spouse as your primary agent and someone close to you, such as a son or daughter, to be your alternate agent.

Why would you need a durable power of attorney? You may be surprised to know that if you do not have one, and you become incompetent, your spouse does not have a legal right to handle your financial affairs. For example, if you have an investment account in your own name (not joint), your spouse will not be allowed to make changes or represent you on the account. The durable power of attorney gives the primary agent the ability to handle your affairs until you die. If you do not have one in place, your spouse must petition the court to be appointed as your guardian. This is not what your spouse will want to be going through if you suddenly become incapacitated. This document is revocable, provided you do it in writing and destroy all existing copies. Please take the steps necessary to put a durable power of attorney into place. An attorney should not charge a lot of money to draft this document.

Advance Directive

An advance directive, also known as a living will or health care directive, is a document that allows you to appoint an agent to make health care decisions on your behalf if you are unable to communicate with your physician or health care team. This document also allows you to give directions to your agent regarding your wishes about what actions or care you would like to receive in certain situations. For example, you can specify where you would like to receive care, provide instructions about artificial feeding, and donate your organs, if that is something you desire.

As with the durable power of attorney, you may revoke the advance directive in writing, stating that you want to cancel it. Make sure you destroy all existing copies if you revoke an advance directive.

By adopting an advance directive, you are relieving your spouse and children of the burden of making some really tough decisions on your behalf. Be sure to have a frank discussion with your family about what your wishes are.

Leave a Roadmap

Can you imagine trying to travel from Florida to California without a map? It would not be very easy, and you probably would take many wrong turns and get off course along the way. That is what it can be like when someone passes away and has not documented the location of their all-important documents. The situation can be especially troublesome if it is the spouse who usually handled the majority of the household's finances and paperwork. I believe one of the best things you can do for your spouse is to *leave a written record of where everything is*. An easy-to-use format follows. Make sure to update it annually to avoid missing recent changes. If some of these items do not apply to you, just skip over them and record what affects your situation.

This letter is reprinted with permission from H.D. Vest Financial Services. Copyright 2001. Statements expressed within this publication should not be considered endorsements of products or procedures by H.D. Vest Financial Services.

Letter to My Loved Ones

From: _____
  Name

Effective: _____ / _____
  Month   *Year*

Dear Loved Ones:

In an attempt to simplify matters for you, I have written this letter to provide you with information that will be necessary for you when the time arises.

Advisors: *Some of the people you will need to contact are listed below:*

Attorney: _____
  Name

_____
Address

_____ _____ _____
City   *State*   *Zip*

_____ _____
Phone   *Fax*

Insurance Advisor: _____
  Name

_____
Address

_____ _____ _____
City   *State*   *Zip*

_____ _____
Phone   *Fax*

Accountant:_____
  Name

_____
Address

_____ _____ _____
City   *State*   *Zip*

_____ _____
Phone   *Fax*

Financial Planner: _____
  Name

_____
Address

_____ _____ _____
City   *State*   *Zip*

_____ _____
Phone   *Fax*

Stockbroker:_____
  Name

_____
Address

_____ _____ _____
City   *State*   *Zip*

_____ _____
Phone   *Fax*

Pension Benefits: _____

Name

_____
Address

_____ _____ _____
City   *State*   *Zip*

_____ _____
Phone   *Fax*

Mortgage Holder: _____

Name

_____
Address

_____ _____ _____
City   *State*   *Zip*

_____ _____
Phone   *Fax*

Employer: _____

Name

_____
Address

_____ _____ _____
City   *State*   *Zip*

_____ _____
Phone   *Fax*

An Act of *Love*

Other: _____
          Name

_____
Address

_____ _____ _____
City   *State*   *Zip*

_____ _____
Phone   *Fax*

Other: _____
          Name

_____
Address

_____ _____ _____
City   *State*   *Zip*

_____ _____
Phone   *Fax*

Other: _____
          Name

_____
Address

_____ _____ _____
City   *State*   *Zip*

_____ _____
Phone   *Fax*

Other: _____
        Name

_____
Address

_____
City   *State*   *Zip*

_____
Phone   *Fax*

Assets:

Here is a list of all my stocks, bonds and other investments, including property. I have listed a contact person and telephone number for each item, as well as the location of any documents. I have _____ have not _____ attached a financial statement.

Investment:

_____
Contact

_____
Phone

_____
Location of documents

Investment:

_____
Contact

_____
Phone

_____
Location of documents

Investment:

_____

Contact

_____

Phone

_____

Location of documents

Investment:

_____

Contact

_____

Phone

_____

Location of documents

Investment:

_____

Contact

_____

Phone

_____

Location of documents

Investment:

_____

Contact

_____

Phone

_____

Location of documents

Investment:

_____
Contact

_____
Phone

_____
Location of documents

Investment:

_____
Contact

_____
Phone

_____
Location of documents

Money is owed to us by:

_____
Contact

_____
Address

_____
Phone

_____
Amount

Money is owed to us by:

_____
Contact

_____
Address

_____
Phone

_____
Amount

Money is owed to us by:

_____
Name

_____
Address

_____
Phone

_____
Amount

Money is owed to us by:

_____
Name

_____
Address

_____
Phone

_____
Amount

Deposits:

I have_____ have not _____ made substantial deposits on certain accounts. If applicable, the accounts are:

_____

_____

_____

_____

Liabilities:

Here is a list of our liabilities, including a contact name and phone number of each, as well as the location of any related documents.

Liability:

_____
Contact

_____
Phone

_____
Location of documents

Liability:

_____
Contact

_____
Phone

_____
Location of documents

Liability:

Contact

Phone

Location of documents

Liability:

Contact

Phone

Location of documents

Liability:

Contact

Phone

Location of documents

Liability:

Contact

Phone

Location of documents

Liability:

Contact

Phone

Location of documents

Liability:

Contact

Phone

Location of documents

Liability:

Contact

Phone

Location of documents

Liability:

Contact

Phone

Location of documents

Liability:

_____
Contact

_____
Phone

_____
Location of documents

Liability:

_____
Contact

_____
Phone

_____
Location of documents

Insurance Coverage:

*I have the following **life insurance** policies (including company owned):*

*For **Type**, use the following: T (Term), VUL (Variable Universal Life), U (Universal Life), W (Whole Life), 2nd (Survivorship Life, also known as Second to Die. If applicable use this code in addition to others listed)*

Any of the policies can be found at

_____	_____	_____
Type	Owner	Beneficiary
$_____	$_____	$_____
Face Amount	Existing Loans	Cash Value

_____ _____ _____
Type   Owner   Beneficiary

$_____ $_____ $_____
Face Amount   Existing Loans   Cash Value

_____ _____ _____
Type   Owner   Beneficiary

$_____ $_____ $_____
Face Amount   Existing Loans   Cash Value

_____ _____ _____
Type   Owner   Beneficiary

$_____ $_____ $_____
Face Amount   Existing Loans   Cash Value

_____.

*I have the following **disability insurance** policies:*

_____
Company

_____
Policy Located at

_____
Company

_____
Policy Located at

_____
Company

_____
Policy Located at

*I have the following **long-term care** policies:*

_____
Company

_____
Policy Located at

_____
Company

_____
Policy Located at

_____
Company

_____
Policy Located at

*I have the following **health insurance** policies:*

_____
Company

_____
Policy Located at

_____
Company

_____
Policy Located at

_____

Company

_____

Policy Located at

I have the following other policies:

Auto:

_____

Company

_____

Policy Located at

Umbrella:

_____

Company

_____

Policy Located at

Home:

_____

Company

_____

Policy Located at

Other:

_____

Company

_____

Policy Located at

Other:

_____

Company

_____

Policy Located at

If I become disabled, please make sure to continue to pay the premiums on the policies, which will provide me or my family benefits.

If I am disabled, my life insurance policy allows ___ does not allow ___ for pre-payment of death benefits to support me.

If I am disabled, my life insurance policy allows ___ does not allow ___ you to stop making premium payments.

If I am disabled, my disability insurance policy allows ___ does not allow ___ you to stop making premium payments.

Employment:

I have the following disability and/or death benefits where I work (briefly describe):

_____
Retirement Plans

_____
Life Insurance

_____
Health Insurance

_____
Long-Term Care Insurance

_____
Disability Insurance

_____

Deferred Compensation

_____

Stock Ownership

_____

Stock Options

_____

Cafeteria Plan

_____

Other

Documents:

I have executed each of the following documents and you can find them where noted:

*Will*_____   _____
                                          Date Signed

_____

Location

*Advanced Directive (Living Will)*___   _____
                                          Date Signed

_____

Location

*Medical Power of Attorney*_____   _____
                                          Date Signed

_____

Location

Medical Directive_____   _____
                                     Date Signed

_____
Location

Durable Power of Attorney_____   _____
                                      Date Signed

_____
Location

Living Trust_____   _____
                                    Date Signed

_____
Location

Insurance Trust_____   _____
                                     Date Signed

_____
Location

Charitable Trust_____   _____
                                     Date Signed

_____
Location

Minor's Trust_____   _____
                                    Date Signed

_____
Location

*Custodial Account*_____ _____
Date Signed

_____
Location

Organ Donation _____ _____
Date Signed

_____
Location

*Pre-Nuptial Agreement*_____ _____
Date Signed

_____
Location

*Post-Nuptial Agreement*_____ _____
Date Signed

_____
Location

*Divorce Decree*_____ _____
Date Signed

_____
Location

*Citizenship Papers*_____ _____
Date Signed

_____
Location

Burial Agreement_____   _____
                                      Date Signed

_____
Location

Retirement Plan Beneficiary Designation _____
                                         Date Signed

_____
Location

Insurance Beneficiary Designation____   _____
                                         Date Signed

_____
Location

I have appointed (in the above documents) the following persons to act in my behalf if I become disabled:

Durable Power of Attorney over my Assets:

1st:_____   2nd:_____

Advance Directive – Medical:

1st:_____   2nd:_____

Guardian over my Property:

1st:_____   2nd:_____

Guardian over my Person:

1st:_____   2nd:_____

It is my desire that the persons having the above powers act on my behalf rather than a guardian being appointed, unless my family believes guardianship is necessary.

In the event of my incapacity, I do ___ do not ___ want to be kept home as long as possible, taking into account the cost.

I have___ do not have___ a divorce decree which may require that certain payments be made after I am disabled or after my death.

General Information:

I do___ do not ___ have a safety deposit box. It can be found at _____ and the key can be found _____.

I do___ do not___ have a personal safe. The combination is _____

The safe can be found: _____
_____.

I have ___ have not ___ attached a list of the persons I want to receive my personal property when I die.

I may receive an inheritance from:

_____

_____

_____

An Act of *Love*

Upon my death, my heirs will ___ will not ___ receive a distribution or benefits from a trust. If yes, the trust instrument was created by: _____

_____.

The trust instrument can be found: _____

_____.

I am ___ am not ___ currently the Trustee for a trust. If I am a Trustee, the trust document is located at:

_____

I am ___ am not ___ a beneficiary of a trust. If I am a beneficiary, the trust document is located at:

_____

My social security number is: _____

My driver's license number is: _____

My passport number is: _____

I am ___ am not ___ entitled to military benefits. List the benefits:

_____

_____

_____

I am ___ am not ___ entitled to other benefits. List the benefits:

_____

_____

_____

In the Event of My Death:

I have the following wishes:

Funeral Home: _____

Cemetery: _____

Plot/Drawer#:_____

I have___ have not___ prepaid my burial cost $____,

for my burial plot $_____ , for my casket $_____.

Information can be found at: _____

_____

I do ___ do not ____ want to be cremated. Crematory:

_____

Minister/Rabbi/Priest to perform service: _____

_____

Pallbearers:

_____   _____

_____   _____

_____   _____

_____   _____

_____   _____

Special Requests:

*Obituary Reading:*_____

_____

_____

_____

Tombstone Engraving: _____

_____

Organs for Donation: _____

_____

In lieu of flowers, please ask for donations to:

_____

_____

Other special requests:

_____

_____

_____

I have signed this family love letter this _____*day of*
_____, _____ *(yr).*
This document is not intended to replace my will or -
other estate planning documents signed by me. How-
ever, it is my express desire that each family member,
Executor, Trustee and Guardian will use this love letter
and the other documents signed by me in making any
discretionary decisions for me and my family.

_____

(sign)

_____ *(print)*

Copies of this document were delivered to:

_____   _____

_____   _____

_____   _____

_____   _____

Review Periodically

Whenever you put a plan in place, you feel a sense of accomplishment and can change your focus to other life issues. That is normal and fine. However, *please remember that you must come back and review your estate plan every five years or when major law revisions are put into place.* Do not rely on your attorney to contact you for this purpose. Attorneys generally do not follow up to review financial and legal plans that have been put in place. If you are in this situation, contact your attorney for a review. You will incur a cost, but it is worth the peace of mind you can achieve knowing your plan will work the way you anticipate. I would also encourage attorneys who do not provide this service to consider contacting their clients and offer them a review.

An example of why this may be a good idea is the changes that have been made to the estate tax laws over the last few years. Many people have the AB trust will that was discussed earlier. When these wills were drafted, they were proper under the laws that existed at the time. The AB trust will states that a trust should be funded to the extent of the applicable exclusion amount. When most of these wills were drafted, the amount was $600,000. Now, because of higher exclusion amounts and the losses people suffered in the stock market, these wills may no longer be appropriate for people who have them. The following is a good example.

When your will was drafted in 1998, your estate was worth $1,200,000. If you had died then, your will would have put $600,000 into a trust and left the other $600,000 outright to your spouse. That made sense. But today (2004) the applicable exclusion amount has risen to $1,500,000. If you die today, your entire estate would go into a trust. This would leave your surviving spouse with no assets in their own name. They would be entitled to the income generated by the trust and have to rely on the trustee of the trust to get any additional funds needed for their education, health, maintenance, and support. If they wanted to spend money on extra items that are outside their typical lifestyle, they would have to convince the trustee to release the funds. This may not be as easy as it sounds because the trustee also has a duty to the principal beneficiaries of the trust and cannot just distribute money based on the surviving spouse's desires.

I do not believe this was the situation people envisioned when they put their AB trust wills in place. Anybody with this type of will should review with their attorney how the current law impacts them. It may mean having a new will (such as a disclaimer will) put in place, but the cost of this would be well worth it when you consider what you may be subjecting the surviving spouse to by not acting. *I urge anyone in this situation to have this reviewed!*

Insurance

Do you have the proper insurance in place to protect your spouse from financial hardship if you were to die or become disabled? Many people do not have the proper amounts of life, disability, or long-term care insurance. This can be caused by not understanding what they need or by a reluctance to pay for something they do not perceive benefits them today. Certainly, the best thing that could happen would be to never collect a penny from insurance policies. However, it is not wise to take such a risk. Obviously, if you hold a life insurance policy long enough you will collect on it. Not collecting on the other types of insurance means you probably missed out on many problems experienced by other people and that is something to be grateful for.

Life Insurance

Should you have life insurance? This is a good question. The answer is "maybe yes" and "maybe no." It depends on each individual's circumstances.

Life insurance is used for different purposes. Some people need it as protection for their spouse and children, wanting to prevent financial hardship if they die prematurely. Others use it to pay estate and income tax at their death, helping to protect their heirs' inheritance. If you are buying life insurance to protect assets, the analysis of how much is needed is different than if you're trying to protect your spouse and children from financial hardship.

When analyzing the amount of life insurance needed to pay estate and income taxes, assuming no business or unusual circumstances are involved, many individuals who are selling life insurance will tell you to buy enough to pay the taxes that will be due. I advise approaching it differently. I ask the individual how much they would like their children to inherit. If you have a $4,000,000 estate and the estate tax would be $1,000,000, your children would inherit $3,000,000. If you have three children, they each would inherit $1,000,000 if they were to share equally. At this point, I ask the individual if they feel their children need to inherit more than $1,000,000. If they say no, I tell them they do not need any life insurance. If they want each child to inherit an extra $333,333, then they should buy the $1,000,000 policy to pay the tax.

If your life insurance need is to prevent financial hardship for your spouse and children, the worksheet in Figure 1 will give you some guidance on the amount you may need. Before purchasing insurance, consult with a professional to make sure the amount you are purchasing makes sense for you and your family.

Figure 1. Life Insurance Worksheet

	Your Information	Sample case
1. **Annual living expenses (use 75% of current living expenses)**		*$50,000*
2. **Continuing income**		
Surviving spouse's salary		*$25,000*
Investment earnings		*$1,000*
Social Security		*$6,000*
Pensions, annuities		*$5,000*
Other income		*$1,000*
Total income (2)		*$38,000*
3. **Annual income shortfall (1–2)**		$12,000
4. **Amount of death benefit needed to generate annual income in Item 3** (item 3 divided by .05)		*$240,000*
5. **Final expenses**		
Funeral, hospital, and medical		*$ 20,000*
Estate settlement costs		*$15,000*
Federal estate taxes		*0*
State estate/ inheritance taxes		*0*
Expense subtotal		*$35,000*

Figure 1 (cont.)

	Your Information	Sample case
Mortgage balance		*$100,000*
College fund		*$50,000*
Total expenses (5)		**$185,000**
6. Preliminary insurance needs (4 + 5)		**$425,000**
7. Existing assets/other insurance		
Existing life insurance		$50,000
Pension and profit sharing		$100,000
Cash and savings		$10,000
Securities		$5,000
IRA and Keogh plans		$30,000
Employer savings plan 401(k)		$20,000
Other liquid assets		$10,000
Total amounts available (7)		**$225,000**
8. Total life insurance needed (6–7)		**$200,000**

There are various types of life insurance. The type you use will be somewhat dictated by what your purpose is. Some types are used for a specific period of time, for accumulating tax-deferred funds, or for funding estate and income tax obligations. Without getting too in-depth, the following lists some major types of insurance and their common uses.

Term Insurance. This insurance is ideal if your need is for a specified period. Term insurance does not build cash value and terminates at the end of a specific time. There are two types of term insurance. The first is an annually **renewable term**, which has a premium that increases each year. When you are younger, this type of insurance provides you with the lowest premiums. As you get older, it can get quite expensive. The second is **level premium term**. This type keeps the premium at a set level for a specified period. For example, you may buy a policy to cover a period of 5 years, 10 years, 20 years, etc. The longer the specified period, the higher the premium will be. Eighty percent of term insurance never pays a death benefit because the policies are allowed to expire.

Whole Life. This type of insurance is permanent or "cash value" insurance, and provides a combination of savings and insurance. The premiums for this type of policy have two components, insurance and savings. In the early years, the cost of the insurance is lower, which allows cash value to build up. In the later years of the policy, the cash value that has built up is used to help offset the higher cost of the insurance and helps continue to increase the cash value of the policy. Premiums are the same amount each year. The earnings inside the policy are compounded tax deferred and are not taxed unless withdrawn from the policy. The insurance company maintains the risk of keeping the policy intact. When the policyholder is older and may not need a large amount of insurance, the cash value can be withdrawn and used as a supplemental source of retirement income. With whole life insurance, your basis in the policy is withdrawn first, so the initial amounts taken are not taxed. If the insurance need still exists, the policy can be kept in force until death.

Universal Life. This is another type of policy that has a cash value. The amounts paid are divided into two pieces. Part of the payment is applied toward the death benefit and part toward the cash value. The policy is flexible because you are not required to pay the same premium every year. If you have a problem paying your premium in one year, you can reduce your payment all the way down to zero. Remember though, the policy must have enough cash value to cover the premium if you do not pay. The policy earnings are usually based on short-term interest rates. The investment risk of this policy lies with the policyholder. Premiums may have to be increased if the cash value is not sufficient to help pay the premiums. In many instances this type of policy is used to pay estate taxes. Another form of this insurance is known as **survivorship (second to die).** Survivorship insures both spouses and will pay a death benefit upon the death of the second spouse. The premium on one survivorship policy will be cheaper than the cost of two individual policies.

Variable Life. In a variable life policy, the savings portion of the premium may be invested in stocks and bonds.

This feature has made this policy popular with younger people who like to use it as a supplemental savings vehicle for retirement. As with universal life, the investment risk lies with the policyholder, and an insufficient cash value may cause the premiums to increase to avoid having the policy lapse. Another form of this insurance is **variable universal life**. This combines the features of both types of policies into one. Before purchasing this type of product you should request a prospectus from your advisor for more complete information about investments, including investment objectives, risks, and charges and expenses. Please read the prospectus and ask questions before you invest.

Disability Insurance

If you are already retired, you do not need disability insurance. However, if you are still working this insurance can be important. If you become disabled you will not only stop bringing home a wage, in most cases you will be incurring medical expenses. Disability insurance may seem expensive, but it is hard to go without.

If you have a policy at your job, good for you. Even so, it would be a good idea to have an insurance professional review your employer's policy to see if you are adequately covered. If you do not have any coverage, you should speak with a professional in this area for advice. You never know when you might be injured. Just look at what happened to the man in the following tale. . .

A man lay sprawled across three seats in a movie theater. The usher came by and said, "Sir, I am going to have to ask you to sit up, you only paid for one and are allowed to use one seat." The man groaned but did not move. The usher was losing his patience and once again said, "Sir, if you do not sit up, I will have to get the owner of the theater." The man just moaned again. With that, the usher stomped off to get the owner. Shortly, he returned with the owner. The two of them tried to get the man to sit up but with no success; he just would not move. Finally, the owner called the police. The policeman arrived and asked the gentleman what his name was. The gentleman said, "George." The policeman said, "Where are you from?" In a pained voice, George replied, "The balcony."

The worksheet that follows (Figure 2) will help you determine the correct amount of disability insurance. You will need to identify your average annual expenses and then determine the amount of income that is needed to pay them. But remember, this is only a guide.

Figure 2. Disability Insurance Worksheet

	Your Information	*Sample Case*
1. Continuing income		
Nondisabled spouse's salary		*$30,000*
Investment earnings		*$2,600*
Other income		*$1,000*
Total income (1)		***$33,600***
2. Annual expenses		
Fixed expenses (fixed expenses include debts and obligations that come due every month)		
Rent or house payment		*$ 18,000*
Taxes and insurance		*$4,000*
Annual house bills (utilities, telephone, cable TV, garbage, water & sewer, etc.)		*$5,800*
Credit card payments		*$3,000*
Auto loan payments		*$4,800*
Other loan payments		*$1,500*
Variable expenses (other expenses that vary from month to month but don't decline significantly with a disability)		
Food		*$6,000*
Clothing		*$4,000*
Transportation		*$4,500*
Miscellaneous expenses		*$6,000*

Figure 2. (cont.)

	Your Information	Sample Case
Total expenses (2)		$57,600
3. Preliminary insurance needs (2–1)		$24,000
4. Monthly benefit needed (3 divided by 12 months)		$2,000
5. Existing disability insurance (employer) monthly benefit		$1,000
6. Monthly disability benefit needed (4–5)		$1,000

Long-Term Care Insurance

Long-term care addresses a person's need for a wide range of medical care, nursing care, and social services over a long period. This is an area that is often overlooked when planning for retirement and for reducing burdens on a spouse.

Planning for long-term care is much more important today than it was 30 or 40 years ago. Back then, life expectancies were shorter, and if someone needed care they would move in with family members who would take care of them. Today most people do not take in their family members, and the cost of care has gotten very expensive. According to the U.S. Census Bureau in 1999, "Individuals 85 years and older, are the fastest growing segment of the population." Along with longer life expectancies comes a greater need for care. The *Wall Street Journal* stated in a June 2000 article: "For 75% of couples aged 65 and older, at least one person will need nursing facility care during their lifetime."

Long-term care insurance has many features and can be a bit complicated, but if you are working with a professional they should be able to simplify things for you. Here is a story that exaggerates the complexity of long-term care insurance.

God granted one wish to an old man who had lived a good life. The man thought for a while and decided that he would like to go to Hawaii. But he was afraid to fly. So he asked God if he would build a bridge from the United States to Hawaii so he could drive. God said this would be a bit difficult and wondered if he had another wish. The man then asked God to explain long-term care insurance to him. God replied, "How many lanes do you want?"

Traditionally, when you think about long-term care, you think about nursing homes. At one time this was true, but today there are many types of long-term care. Now one of the most popular types of long-term care is *home health care.* The majority of people who need long-term care would prefer to be able to stay home and receive it. This has been made possible by health care workers who will deliver services to you in your home. Medical professionals, from physicians to physical therapists, will come to your house for an hourly rate and provide you with the services you require. In addition, you can hire people to clean, cook, and assist you with the smaller day-to-day tasks that at one time might have required a nursing home stay.

Another type of care that is getting popular is *assisted living*. Assisted living promotes independence, incorporating a combination of housing, personal care services, and health care. Thus the living environment is set up so that an individual can maintain their independence for as long as possible. Think of it as moving into your own apartment with a full kitchen and everything you need to live independently. However, if you like, the facility will provide you with any of the services you may need: cooking, cleaning, laundry, etc. You only pay for the services you decide to use. Generally, assisted living residences also have transportation available for shopping and entertainment events. They may even have their own in-house entertainment and social events. As time goes on and you need more in-depth care they will provide it. In fact, some of them are combined with full-service nursing homes. An assisted living facility is a good option to explore.

Other types of care include *adult day care* and *residential care*. Adult day care is a drop-in service, providing a place for you to take the person you are caring for when you need to work, run errands, or take a break. They charge by the day or by the hour, and operate a bit like a childcare facility. Residential care is provided in a home setting and generally has only five or six residents. These facilities often provide top-notch care but are usually quite expensive.

According to the American Council of Life Insurers the average annual cost for long-term care in a nursing home is $55,000; home health care, $30,000; and assisted living facilities, $26,300. When planning for long-term care, it is essential that you know how you will be paying for this expense. I can think of three ways.

The first is to be poor and let the government pay for it. The government has two programs, Medicaid and Medicare. To qualify for Medicaid you need to reduce your assets to the poverty level. This may be the right thing to do if you do not have many assets to begin with. To qualify for Medicaid you cannot have more than a small amount of assets determined on a state-by-state basis. Many states allow the spouse who needs medical assistance to keep $2,000–$3,000. The other spouse may keep a limited amount of assets (usually less than $100,000), which do not include the family home or automobile. Rules exist to try to prevent individuals from gifting their assets away in order to qualify. In some situations, through creative planning with an elder law attorney, people have been able to qualify even if they have had a large amount of assets. But, there is no guarantee this would work for you. If you think this is an avenue you would like to explore, I would suggest you work with an elder law attorney.

The Medicare program is not meant to be a long-term care program. It will provide some coverage for long-term care but only a limited amount. The government will pay

100% of the first 20 days of your stay and the amount over $105 for days 21 thru 100. As you can see, these benefits only last a short period of time and can't be counted on long-term. To qualify for this limited benefit you must have a three-night stay in a hospital and then be discharged by a doctor to a nursing home. For the coverage to continue, you must be rehabilitating while you are in the nursing home. If at any time you stop improving and your care becomes custodial in nature, Medicare will stop payments. The bottom line is you cannot rely on Medicare for long-term care.

The second way to pay for long-term care is to use your own assets, if you have enough. This is fine if you can afford it, but for many people such expenses are prohibitive. You may have $500,000 in the bank and feel good about this amount, but it may not be enough. What if you have to pay an annual nursing home bill of $55,000 and also continue to support the spouse that stays at home? Your money will run out quicker than you think. If your money was earning 5% annual interest and you had to pay $55,000 for nursing home care and $25,000 for your spouse to stay at home, your money would not even last eight years. No one can tell you what the magic number is, but a good financial planner can help you work through some scenarios and determine if you can afford to pay for this need on your own.

The third funding approach is to buy long-term care insurance. For many people, I believe this is the right answer. We insure our cars, homes, and lives, yet the type of insurance that may be most likely used is not purchased. In September 2002, State Farm Insurance commissioned a Roper poll to determine consumers' concerns about long-term care insurance. The study found that only 17% of American adults owned a long-term care policy. Hopefully, this statistic will improve, because if it doesn't it is likely that a lot of people will be paying for their own care with the risk of impoverishing their stay-at-home spouse. Believe me, paying a long-term care premium of $1,500 a year is a lot cheaper that paying an annual fee of $55,000 to a nursing home or paying any of the other types of long-term care discussed earlier.

The major reason to buy a long-term care policy is to protect your family's finances. Another reason is that a lot of people want to maintain their independence and avoid being dependent on or a burden to their children. Preserving assets for other purposes may also be a reason. I worked with an individual who wanted to pay a grandchild's education costs in college and medical school. This was very possible as long as she did not need long-term care services. She bought a policy to protect against this, and she was no longer fearful of being unable to pay for her grandchild's education.

Another big reason to buy long-term care insurance is to eliminate the "what-if" cloud. I have met with several people who have a net worth of $500,000 or more, and the one issue that kept them up at night was "what-if?" What if one of the spouses had to begin receiving long-term care services? Although they were currently comfortable with their financial situation, they knew that if one of them had an extended period of need for long-term care services their financial picture was in jeopardy. These were people who could well afford to pay the premiums. Some decided to purchase a policy, and others are probably still staying awake at night worrying about "what if." While buying a long-term care policy does not guarantee financial freedom, it certainly should allow you to rest easier.

How is the cost of a long-term care policy determined? The insurance company considers many factors. Some of the most important are age, health history, and the policy benefits you choose. You can't do much about your age and your health may also be hard to change. But you can control the cost of the policy depending on which benefits you elect.

The major benefits that you need to consider are:

1. Daily benefit
2. Elimination period
3. Length of benefit
4. Inflation rider
5. Home health care option

The *daily benefit* defines how much you want the insurance company to reimburse you for your care. The average daily cost of a nursing home is $150. Why would you not just buy a policy with a $150 daily benefit? Because this may be more benefit than you need. The following worksheet (Figure 3) will give you a quick way to estimate the benefit that may be appropriate for you. Remember, *before purchasing a policy discuss the reason you chose a certain daily benefit with your insurance professional.*

Figure 3. Long-Term Care Worksheet

	Your Information	*Sample Case*
1. Continuing income		
Spouse's salary		*$25,000*
Investment earnings		*$10,000*
Social Security		*$13,500*
Pensions, annuities		*$5,000*
Other income		*$1,000*
Total income (1)		*$54,500*
2. Annual living expenses (use 75% of current living expenses)		*$36,000*
3. Long-term care cost		*$55,000*
4. Total funding need (2 + 3)		*$91,000*
5. Shortfall (4–1)		*($36,500)*
Daily benefit needed (item 5 divided by 365)		*$100*

The *elimination period* is comparable to a deductible amount. In other words, this is the amount you will be responsible for. You can choose a variety of elimination periods. It could be 0 days, 30 days, 90 days, 1 year, etc. For example, if you choose an elimination period of 90 days you will be responsible for paying the first 90 days of coverage, and your policy will begin to pay on day 91. Why would you choose a longer elimination period? Simple—the longer the elimination period, the lower the premium.

The *length of benefit* defines for what period the policy will pay benefits. The period you choose will affect the cost—the longer the benefit period, the more the policy will cost. How long of a benefit do you need? I usually advise people to buy a benefit period of five years or longer. This is a longer time period than the average nursing home stay. According to a study completed by the MetLife Mature Market Institute in 2003, the average nursing home stay is 2.4 years. The study did not consider whether there was some home health care utilized before entering the nursing home.

An *inflation rider* helps the policy benefit keep up with price increases. It is essential that you choose an inflation rider for your policy. Generally, two choices are offered: a simple or a compound rider. The inflation riders increase the policy benefit by 5% a year. The simple rider increases the policy benefit by 5% of the original benefit each year. If your daily benefit is $100, the increase will be $5 ($100 x 5%) every year. If you elect the compound rider, the benefit will increase at a faster pace because the increase is compounded. For example, if you buy a $100 benefit, the increase in the first year will be $5 ($100 x 5%). The second year would be $5.25 ($105 x 5%). Generally, if you are in your seventies or older I would suggest buying a simple rider because a compound rider can get quite expensive. If you are in your sixties or younger, you should strongly consider using a compound rider.

Home health care is a standard feature of most policies issued today. You can purchase a home health care option at 50%, 75%, 100%, etc. I believe the 100% home heath care option is best. After all, home is where most people would like to be cared for, so why would you not want 100% coverage? The only exception would be a single person who does not have anyone at home to assist them and would require 24-hour-a-day home health care. This could be quite expensive, but if you can afford it, buy a higher home health care option such as 130%.

When should you buy a long-term care policy? I do not think there is a correct answer. I suggest people purchase policies when they are in their fifties for two different reasons. First, the cost of the policy is more affordable at this age. Second, your chances of qualifying are much better than if you wait. The longer you wait the more likely you are to develop a condition that will disqualify you from getting a policy. My experience shows that when you reach your seventies, it is very difficult to qualify. Does this mean if you are seventy you should not apply? The answer is no—everybody's situation is different—but you need to understand that getting a policy at this age is not a sure thing.

As you can tell, I like long-term care insurance. Obviously, it will not be a good answer if you cannot afford it. The worksheet in Figure 4 is a guide to help you determine if you can afford it. You and your spouse, along with your insurance professional, must make the final determination.

Figure 4. Long-Term Care Worksheet—Can You Afford It?

	Your Information	*Sample Case*
1. Family income		
Investment earnings Total investments multiplied by 5% (assumed $500,000 of investments)		*$25,000*
Social Security		*$19,000*
Pensions, annuities		*$8,000*
Other income		*$1,000*
Total income (1)		***$53,000***
2. Annual living expenses		***$45,000***
3. Net income available (2 – 1)		***$8,000***

The net income available in the example above is $8,000. Because unexpected expenses will come up from time to time, keep $3,000 available to handle these situations. This would leave $5,000 available to pay for long-term care premiums. The mistake most people make when trying to determine what they can afford is to look at the cash flow generated by their investments instead of the total return. If interest is being reinvested, you may not count it as income but you should. It is money that could be spent without reducing the principal of your investments.

One last thought about how to pay for long-term care insurance. Many people have life insurance policies they have owned for many years, and the policies' cash values have built up. In many cases, the original reason for owning the policy is gone. You may want to consider utilizing the cash in these policies to pay for your long-term care premiums. Remember, however, that these policies may have surrender charges still in effect, so you would need to verify this with the insurance company. In addition, some of these policies may have a taxable gain built into them, but there are methods available that would allow you to defer the gains. The tax code allows something known as a *Section 1035 tax-free exchange*. Under this provision, a life insurance cash value can be exchanged tax free into an annuity. There are many types of annuities defined in the "Annuities" section of Chapter 26, "Investments," in Part III. One type is an immediate annuity. An *immediate annuity* pays a guaranteed monthly amount (based on the insurance company's ability to pay) to the purchaser based on age and current interest rates. As you receive the annuity payments each year, you would pay tax on a portion of the payment designated as income from investments in the annuity. The amount left over after paying the tax could be used to help pay your long-term care premium. The money was originally intended for life insurance; now you are redirecting those dollars to pay for long-term care. Make sure you understand what types of fees and expenses are associated with annuities before making a purchase.

When determining if you can afford a long-term care policy, you have to consider if you can afford future increases in premiums. Even though the annual premium originally quoted to you is presented as an annual payment, the insurance company can raise the premium. To increase the premium, the insurance company must raise the premium for everyone who owns the same policy. They cannot single you out and raise only your premium. To date, not many companies have raised their premiums, but I believe the industry is still fairly young, so the true rate of likely future price increases is not yet known.

If you do decide to purchase a policy, make sure that you are working with a qualified insurance professional and only purchase a policy from a strong company with good financial ratings. The A.M. Best Company and Standard and Poors Corp. are two organizations that rate insurance companies. Try to purchase policies that are rated A or better by A.M. Best Company or AA- or better by Standard and Poors Corp.

Obviously, the longer you maintain your good health, the longer you may be able to put off needing these insurances. Therefore, following a sensible diet and getting regular exercise makes good sense. If you are having health problems, make an appointment to see a doctor. Just make sure the appointment is for the right person, unlike the person in this joke. . .

An older gentleman was afraid that his wife was losing her hearing. One day he called the doctor and made an appointment to have her hearing checked. The appointment was set for two weeks out. The doctor told the man that in the meantime he could give his wife a simple test to help the doctor understand the extent of the problem. He instructed the man to stand about 40 feet away from his wife and ask her a question in a normal tone to see if she could hear him. If she did not reply, he was to repeat the test from 30 feet, then 20 feet and so on until she responded. That night, while his wife was in the kitchen cooking, he walked to the other side of the house until he was 40 feet away and in a normal voice said, "Sweetheart, what are you cooking?" He heard no response so he moved 30 feet away and tried again. He still heard no response. Then he went to 20 feet and then 10 feet. Finally, standing in the doorway a few feet away, he repeated the question. She finally turned around and said, "Darn it, Earl, for the fifth time it is chicken!"

Business Succession Planing

If either spouse owns all or part of a business, you need to have a plan in place to sell the business if the involved spouse passes away or becomes disabled. Many times people who own a business have most of their assets tied up in the business and look at it as their retirement plan. This asset needs to be protected for the surviving spouse, as it may be their only source of income. They could not survive without the income from the business or manage even an interruption in the cash flow.

Receiving full value for a business is very difficult if you have to sell it after a key person dies or becomes disabled. If your spouse is an owner with other people, it is unlikely that they would want you as a partner or that you would like to be their partner because, in most situations, the spouse who is not involved in the business does not have either the interest or the expertise to continue the business.

The most common tool used for selling a business under these circumstances is known as a *buy-sell agreement.*

A buy-sell agreement is an agreement to buy or sell a business at a determinable price under certain terms upon the occurrence of an event such as a death or disability. It allows you to specify what happens to your business if you pass away; and if there are multiple owners, it allows each person to know what will happen should one of the owners leave the business. Because the terms are agreed to in advance, the agreement greatly reduces arguments or disagreements when it must be used. Generally, an attorney drafts a buy-sell agreement.

The agreement will identify who has the right to purchase the business and how the price will be determined. Many times the agreement is funded using life insurance proceeds or a savings account known as a "sinking fund." Life insurance is generally purchased in an amount large enough to purchase the insured's share of the business. If a savings account is used, it may or may not be large enough to fund the total purchase price of the business. Whatever amount is in the account can be applied toward the purchase of the business interest. The major benefits of having this type of agreement include:

- Provides for the continuation of the business without interruption

- Provides support for the family of the deceased owner

- Generates cash to pay estate taxes and estate settlement costs
- Provides a formula to value the business
- Allows the owners of the business to identify who their future partners will be

Terminal Illness

Likely the most difficult message you will ever hear from your doctor is that you have a limited amount of time to live. You may be told that you have 6 weeks, 6 months, or a year; it does not matter, coming to grips with this reality is hard to imagine. The emotional impact will be hard on you and your family, and you must do your best to deal with it. In addition, financial issues will come into play, and while they may not seem like a top priority in light of how you are feeling, they cannot be ignored.

The first step is to understand what the financial impact of the illness will be. Talk to doctors or organizations that have ties to the specific illness you are dealing with. When you have a feel for what costs may be involved, contact your insurance company to determine if your policy will cover the services required. If you find out that not all of the costs will be covered, review your budget and cash flows to determine how you will pay for the portion you are responsible for. You also might want to consider reviewing your investments and repositioning them if it is likely you will need cash and your current portfolio is not liquid.

If you are working, and you are able to continue working you may want to consider keeping your job because your employer may provide financial and medical benefits that could help you. Some people want to keep working to keep their mind off their illness. If you do decide to leave your employer, you will want to utilize *COBRA*. COBRA is federal law passed in 1985 that guarantees you the right to continue your former employer's group plan for individual or family health insurance for up to 18 months at your own expense. If you are disabled at the time you leave your job, the 18 months is extended by 11 months to a total of 29 months. In many cases, your spouse and dependent children are also eligible for COBRA coverage, sometimes for as long as three years.

If you have a disability insurance policy, you will want to review it to see what benefits you are eligible to receive. If you are really in need of cash, some life insurance policies will allow you to receive some of your death benefit early. This is commonly referred to as an "accelerated benefit."

If at this point you do not have your estate planning documents in place, now is the time you must take action. Please review Chapter 4 on estate planning and contact an attorney about taking the appropriate steps.

Beneficiary Designations

An easy area to overlook, but an important one, is beneficiary designations. A beneficiary designation that is wrong can have disastrous ramifications. An attorney I have worked with tells the story about one of his clients who was divorced years ago and had remarried. He failed to change the beneficiary on a major life insurance policy. When he passed away, his widow was expecting to collect the benefits on a large life insurance policy that she needed for support. Well, she got the surprise of her life when she found out he had failed to change the beneficiary on the policy. His first wife was still listed as the beneficiary and she collected the insurance proceeds, leaving the new widow in a tough situation. This story shows how important it is to check your beneficiary designations from time to time to make sure they are current and designated as you intended.

In most situations, you will want to have your spouse listed as your beneficiary. However, there are times you may use others. The following are times when you may not want to use your spouse:

- This may be a second marriage for you and, depending on your wife's financial condition, you might designate your children from a first marriage as beneficiaries of your retirement plan.

- Your estate may be large and subject to estate tax. Planning may dictate that you leave your retirement plan proceeds directly to your children because your spouse already has a taxable estate.

- In some estate planning cases, life insurance will be left to the estate to help one spouse utilize their applicable exclusion amount (see Chapter 4).

- If your estate is large and you have life insurance owned by an irrevocable life insurance trust, you would name the trust the beneficiary.

One word of caution: *do not use your estate as the beneficiary designation on your IRAs or retirement plans.* This could have unintended tax consequences for your estate. The income tax could become due much more quickly than you would like.

Other than the exceptions just listed, your spouse should be the primary beneficiary and your children should be the secondary beneficiaries. And be sure that every few years you review the beneficiary designations on your IRAs, retirement plans, life insurance policies, and any other applicable financial documents. If you are unsure about the best beneficiary designation for your situation, consult with your financial advisor.

Funerals

An important piece of planning for your spouse relates to funerals. You may be wondering why funerals are being discussed since they do not take place until after you pass away. What you may not know is funerals can be planned in advance. This chapter will address various funeral issues but the major focus will be funeral preplanning, which is an important component of preparing your spouse for life without you.

Funeral Preplanning

No one likes to think about death, but if it is your goal to make it easier on your surviving spouse, preplanning a funeral makes a lot of sense. When a spouse dies, you will be faced with numerous decisions. Which funeral home will you use? Should you consider cremation or have a traditional burial? What kind of casket should you choose? What other arrangements need to be considered? How much is it going to cost? What makes this so difficult are that these decisions need to be made right away. You do not have the luxury of going home and thinking about it for a week. Add to this the fact that these decisions have to be made while an individual and family are experiencing great stress and grief, and you may understand why preplanning makes sense.

A funeral director I know told me a story about someone who always had intended to do preplanning for his family, but had failed to do so. He waited too long, a death occurred, and he was the executor of the estate, responsible for making the funeral arrangements. At the last minute, he was still rushing around finalizing things. When he arrived for the wake, he realized he had on one brown shoe and one black shoe. He had been rushing about and put on the wrong shoes. Luckily, the funeral director wore the same size shoe and was able to come to the rescue. This is just an example of how last minute stress can affect a person. Preplanning should help avoid added and unnecessary stress during a difficult time.

By preplanning your funeral, you are making one of the hardest events people ever experience just a little easier. Funeral preplanning provides many advantages:

- *Peace of mind.* Each spouse can rest easy knowing that when one of them passes away the survivor has a plan to follow and will not have to make these decisions while grieving.

- *Eliminates uncertainty.* Because you were involved with the planning, the surviving spouse and family knows that your wishes are being carried out. This avoids the need for them to guess at what you may have wanted.

- *Decisions are more emotionally sound.* Because the decisions are made in the comfort of your own home, they are thought through more thoroughly.

- *Cost control.* Many times decisions made at the time of death can result in overspending due to emotions. You will make better financial decisions when you are not under stress or experiencing shock or grief.

If you do make funeral prearrangements, make sure you inform your family and advise them of where you are storing the related documents. This information can be recorded in the "Letter to My Loved Ones" which can be found in the section titled "Leave a Roadmap" in Chapter 4 in Part I.

Selecting a Funeral Home

The first step in preplanning a funeral is to choose a funeral services provider to work with. You will want to consider location, reputation, and cost. What is the best way to find one? Some of the funeral homes in your area are probably familiar to you. You may have seen advertisements or driven by funeral homes and their names will be familiar. If not, you could check the yellow pages or the Internet. Or you may seek a referral from friends.

You also should talk with the managers of more than one funeral home to see who you are most comfortable with. When checking on cost, find out what you get for the price. Make sure you are comparing apples to apples. The price of one provider may include services not provided by another. Ask what the price includes. (See "The Funeral Rule" on page 105 for more information on being an informed consumer of funeral home services.)

How to Preplan a Funeral

The first thing many people do is purchase a plot in the cemetery where they would like to be buried. Many times a married couple will purchase both of their plots at the same time to ensure they are together. It is not unusual for people to know where they would like to be buried because they may have a family history of using a certain cemetery. If you do not, you will need to identify where you would like to be buried. This may take some visits to cemeteries to find the one you are comfortable with. Items that you should consider are the cost, location, cemetery restrictions, and if it meets your religious and aesthetic requirements. You will purchase the lot directly from the cemetery.

After purchasing a cemetery lot and choosing a funeral services provider, the next step is to meet with the funeral director to choose the type of funeral that you desire. This is when you choose the type of merchandise: casket, vault, cremation, container, urn, type of service, and all of the other items you would desire for your funeral. The funeral provider has been through this many times and will assist you through this process.

After planning your funeral, you will have to decide how you will pay for the service. The cost of your funeral will depend on the type of funeral you planned and the merchandise you selected. The costs can be broken down into three areas:

1. **Funeral and staff charges.** Includes fees for funeral planning, preparation and filing of permits, death certificates, consulting with cemetery or crematory, etc.

2. **Services and merchandises.** Includes cost of casket and vault, embalming, use of funeral home, memorial service, cremation or interment, etc.

3. **Cash advances.** Includes flowers, obituary notices, clergy, organists, soloist honorariums, etc.

Your funeral may be paid in a variety of ways. The two most common methods are known as the bank trust or funeral trust and funeral insurance.

- **Bank trust or funeral trust.** In this method, funds generally equal to the cost of the funeral at today's prices are placed in a funeral trust account at a bank and invested in interest-bearing investments. The hope is that the interest your account earns will keep up with inflation affecting funeral costs. This method can be used by anyone, but it does make more sense for some than others. If you have been given a limited time to live and your period will be relatively short, normally less than one year, this method makes sense. This method may also be a good option for you if you have an illness that would render you uninsurable. One drawback to the funeral trust is that the interest earned by the trust fund is subject to income tax and will be reported to you annually on a Federal Form 1099.

- **Funeral insurance.** Funeral funding using this method is accomplished by purchasing a life insurance policy on the life of the person planning the funeral. The policy is customized for preneed purposes and directs the payment of the death benefit to the funeral home upon death. Normally, the beginning death benefit is equal to the cost of the funeral at today's prices. These policies earn interest or have some type of inflation protection built into them to keep up with the possible increase in funeral cost caused by inflation. Because a life insurance policy is being used, any earnings on the policy are not taxable. They can be established as a single premium payment policy or set up on a payment plan basis over a term of years.

Another option that is available when preplanning your

funeral is to guarantee the cost of the funeral. There are both guaranteed and nonguaranteed options.

- **Guaranteed.** The merchandise, facilities, and services you select will have their cost guaranteed by the funeral home. This relieves you of having to worry about prices increasing. The money you deposit plus earnings or life insurance you purchased will go to the funeral home as payment-in-full. The guarantee does not cover the items categorized as "cash advances" (see previous description). If these items cost more than the original quote, the funeral home can charge the extra cost but not more than the actual cost of these items.

- **Nonguaranteed.** At the time of the funeral, the actual costs incurred are what must be paid. If the amounts in the trust account or the life insurance proceeds are in excess of the actual cost, you receive a refund. Otherwise, you must pay the difference between the cost and the money available.

Funeral Prepayment and Medicaid Planning

Many people will rely on Medicaid to pay for their long-term care in a nursing home. As stated earlier in the discussion of long-term care planning, to qualify you must spend your assets down to $2,000–$3,000 (depending on your state of residence). Certain transfers are considered nonqualifying, such as making large gifts to family and friends. Prepayment of a funeral, however, counts as a qualifying transfer and should be a part of any plan involving spending down your assets to qualify for Medicaid assistance.

The Funeral Rule

The FTC (Federal Trade Commission) along with individual states have the responsibility of regulating the funeral industry. On April 30, 1984, the Funeral Rule, which was developed by the FTC, took effect. The Funeral Rule is a list of requirements that must be adhered to by funeral providers. The rule was developed to protect consumers shopping for a funeral. The major points of the rule are as follows:

- Requires a written, itemized general price list be given to you for your retention.

- Providers must show you descriptions and prices of caskets and outer burial containers before actually showing you the merchandise.

- Many providers offer "funeral packages," but you have the right to buy individual goods and services and refuse a package that may include items you do not want.

- Providers may not falsely state that embalming is required and must disclose in writing that, except in certain cases, the law does not require embalming.

◆ Providers may not state that a casket is required for direct cremation, because it is not.

These are the major points that consumers should be aware of from the Funeral Rule. The FTC has published a consumer's guide called *Funerals—A Consumer Guide*. See the guide for a further explanation of the Funeral Rule. To obtain the guide, call the FTC at 1-877-382-4357 or go to their Web site at www.ftc.gov and print a copy.

Plan Carefully

Funeral preplanning is a service provided by trustworthy professionals, but you still need to be careful. It is critically important that you select a provider whom you trust and have confidence in. As in most industries, shady characters exist, so the buyer must beware. The following six questions are taken from the FTC's *Funerals—A Consumer Guide* and should be asked if you are preplanning a funeral.

1. What are you are paying for? Are you buying only merchandise, like a casket and vault, or are you purchasing funeral services as well?

2. What happens to the money you have prepaid? (States have different requirements for handling funds paid for prearranged funeral services.)

3. What happens to the interest income on money that is prepaid and put into a trust account?

4. Are you protected if the firm goes out of business?

5. Can you cancel the contract and get a full refund if you change your mind?

6. What happens if you move to a different area or die while away from home? (Some prepaid funeral plans can be transferred, but often at an added cost.)

Getting answers to these questions should give you a better understanding of what you are buying and how you are protected.

Final Thoughts on Funeral Preplanning

A few preplanning tips issued by the National Research and Information Center are good reminders:

- Make sure the plan you choose secures your funds

- Make sure your plan is flexible

- Get everything in writing

- Read and reread each part of the contract

- Do not sign anything before you understand it

- Give copies to your family

- Keep a copy in a safe place readily accessible to your survivors (e.g., not in a safety deposit box)

- If so desired, review your plan periodically to ensure it is correct

I hope that this information will allow you to success-
fully preplan your funeral.

Social Issues

I believe that people who are more connected socially with friends and have group involvement have the best chance for a healthy and satisfying life as widows. If all of your activities are tied to one person and that person ceases to exist it can be extremely difficult. When you have too much time on your hands you may have a tendency to dwell on the unfortunate events that have occurred and not have enough distractions to help you focus on the positives and look to the future.

If you do not have a lot of friends or group involvement, and most of your social life is tied to your spouse, now is the best time to change. Many opportunities exist to get involved with groups. You may want to find out what type of activities your current friends or other family members are involved in and inquire about joining these groups.

For people who are members of a church, many different groups are usually available. Look at the bulletin boards or ask other members for information. Many churches also do volunteer work, like helping out at local food shelters or other well-deserving operations. You not only can get satisfaction by helping, but you will also get to know other volunteers, and you may find a new friend!

Do you have hobbies that you currently do now with your spouse or did in the past? For example, do you golf or bowl? Find a league to join where you can meet other people who like to do these same things. Maybe you like to play cards or read books; find a card or book club to join. Any one of these activities will get you involved with other people who have a common interest and the potential for friendship.

If you like to learn, you could enroll in some classes that interest you at the local community education center. Keeping in shape is important for everyone; maybe a local health club would be interesting to you. There are so many possibilities, you only need to take a little effort and search them out. Remember, it is easier to do these things now while your spouse is alive. Once you are a widow you may be emotionally unsure of yourself and lose some confidence. Now is the time to do it!

Being Prepared

I believe if you implement the suggestions discussed to this point, you and your spouse may be much better prepared for the inevitable day when one of you passes away. Many people avoid this type of planning because it forces them to deal with their own mortality. Nevertheless, preparing for the inevitable will not cause it to occur any sooner than not preparing for it. And implementing the proper plan should leave you with a feeling of "being prepared," knowing you did all you could to help the person you love the most prepare for what may be some of their most difficult days.

Ready or Not

Activities Needed Within Nine Months of Death

You must do the things you think you cannot do.

—*Eleanor Roosevelt*

After the funeral is over many decisions will still need to be made and many issues dealt with. It is normal to feel overwhelmed by the tasks ahead of you. You are grieving and may not feel mentally ready to begin. Fortunately, the majority of financial decisions do not have to be addressed right away. In fact, it is wise to move slowly when dealing with major financial decisions.

However, several issues will need to be handled immediately. Most important, you will need to complete these tasks. They cannot be done by others on your behalf. While you do not need to start the day after the funeral, you should begin within 30 days after your loss.

Gather Important Documents

An essential first step is to gather all of your important papers together. This task will be much easier if you have a good filing system as suggested in Part I. These documents include:

- your spouse's will or living trust

- marriage certificate

- life insurance policies

- military discharge papers

- both spouses Social Security cards

- birth certificates for the entire family

These documents will be needed to support your claims for life insurance, social security, employer benefits, and veteran's benefits, and for securing copies of the death certificate. Ideally, all of these important papers were stored in a central location where they can be easily retrieved. If this is not the case, you will need to check in places where it is likely you would file important papers. It could be a safety deposit box, a drawer, a banker's box, or any other location where you and your spouse had a habit of filing documents. Naturally you don't have to do this on your own, and may ask a friend or loved one to assist you with the search.

If your search does not result in finding all of these papers, you will need to do some more work. The attorney who drafted your will would certainly have retained a copy for their files. If you are searching for a life insurance policy, many life insurance companies send annual statements, although some do not. Also, you may be able to look through your current and old check registers to see if payments were being made to an insurance company.

Safety Deposit Box

Another location to search for important documents would be your safety deposit box. In most states, if the box was rented only in the name of your spouse, it will require a court order to open the box. Only a will, trust, or any materials pertaining to the death can be removed before the will is probated. However, if you are a co-signer on the box, you may legally have access to the box and remove anything you wish. If you are a co-signer on the box, go to the bank where the box is located, taking with you the key, a briefcase or bag, and a pencil and paper. If any of the documents listed earlier are in the box, remove them.

Make a list of any items that you leave in the box. Set up a file folder labeled "Safety Deposit Box" and store your list in it in a central filing location where you will be keeping all of your files (as described in Chapter 1, "Record Keeping," in Part I).

Obtaining Death Certificates

The first task to pursue before the business and legal issues can begin is to obtain certified copies of the death certificate. Generally, it is a good idea to order two dozen. You will likely be required to provide them to everyone who is involved with your financial and property ownership issues. In most situations, a certified copy of the death certificate will be requested, so you cannot send photocopies. Store your certified copies in a file folder to make it easy to access them when needed.

Death certificates can be obtained from the registrar of vital statistics in the county where your spouse died. Most often, the funeral director can order as many copies as you will need and may have already taken care of this for you.

Paying Bills

Whatever you do, continue to pay your bills. Although you are still filled with grief, bill paying is essential. It may seem easier to file the bills and pay them later, but it is an action you will come to regret. Late payments can result in penalties, interest and a bad mark on your credit record. Sad to say, but some creditors will not be as sympathetic as you would hope.

First, determine the amount of money in the checking account and make a note of it. Next, gather all of your bills together. Then write down the debtor, the amount due, and the minimum payment due. You may want to pay the minimum due at this time until you get a better handle on the finances. Naturally, you must make sure the amount in your checkbook is large enough to cover the amount of the bills that you want to pay.

Carefully scrutinize the bills that are in your spouse's name only to be sure they are legitimate. If the bill looks unfamiliar, do not pay it. When in doubt, write the creditor and ask for proof that the claim is valid. Unscrupulous people will take advantage of widows by sending bills and demanding payment for services or goods never received by your spouse. Unfortunately, this is not an uncommon scam.

Legal Issues

What is an Estate?

When a person passes away, an estate is created. The estate is a separate legal and taxable entity. It is created at the date of death without regard to other activities that may be taking place, such as appointing a personal representative or probating the will. The estate includes all property owned at death. The estate continues in existence until all of the duties required to be performed by the executor or personal representative have been completed. These duties generally include gathering the assets, paying debts, and distributing the net estate according to the will. This process, on average, could take 18–24 months, depending on the complexity of the estate and whether or not probate is involved.

Wills, Trusts, and Intestacy

Generally, an estate will be directed and settled in one of three ways. First, if your spouse had a will, it will dictate how the estate is to be distributed, and there is a good chance that the probate process will be engaged. Second, if a living trust was in force at death, the settlement process will normally be simpler than if a will was in place. Probate will be avoided if the decedent's assets were titled properly. Third, if the deceased did not have a trust or a will, they will have died intestate. This is the least desirable of the three options. The estate, then, will likely be distributed according to the applicable state law of intestacy. A court-appointed administrator, who is required to follow the state rules on distributions, handles the estate settlement. Regardless of your situation, a visit with an attorney will save you and the beneficiaries of the estate much time, money, and effort later.

Obtaining Legal Help

Contacting an attorney soon after the funeral is essential. There are many legal issues that you will face and need assistance with. The attorney will be able to answer many of your questions and simplify many of the problems you may face. If you are not comfortable visiting an attorney alone, bring along a friend or adult child whose opinion you value. This may help reassure you that the choice you make is the correct one.

Selecting an Attorney

You may already have an attorney you are working with. If not, your first choice would likely be the attorney who drafted your spouse's will or trust. This person will usually be in the best position to assist you with the settlement of your spouse's estate. If your spouse did not have a will or the drafting attorney is no longer practicing, you will need to find a new one.

Part I, Chapter 4, "Estate Planning for Married Couples," provides some sources for finding an attorney. The attorney you select should have experience in estate settlement. It would be best if the attorney specialized in this area. You do not want to be paying someone to get educated on estate administration while they are working on your spouse's estate.

When you meet with a prospective attorney, you should ask certain questions:

- How many years of experience do you have in estate administration?

- What credentials do you have to support your professional status?

- Which professional organizations do you belong to?

- How much of your continuing education is focused on estate settlement?

- What are the tasks that need to be performed?

- How will you keep me informed of the progress of the job?

- How much will it cost?

What is the Cost?

It is very important that you have an estimate of the legal cost you will likely incur. Attorneys charge in many different ways. They may charge on an hourly basis, a flat fee, or in some states, it may be a percent of the estate. You need to know how you will be charged. Before meeting with an attorney, ask if the initial meeting will be free, so that both parties can consider whether they would like to work together. Find out if a retainer (down payment for services) is required. In my opinion, it is best to hire the attorney on an hourly basis for estate administration work. Most important, request a fee quote for all work to be performed.

Working with Your Attorney

Before beginning to work with your attorney, you will need to agree on the work to be done and the price. Many attorneys use a letter of engagement. This letter should spell out the tasks to be performed and the estimated costs. In addition, it should lay out the responsibilities of all the involved parties.

You should also ask to meet all the people in the office who may be involved in your case. This is important, because at times it may be difficult for you to reach the attorney. You need someone else you can contact. Generally, the paralegal working with the attorney will be knowledgeable and able to assist you. In addition, the hourly rate of the paralegal will be lower than that of the attorney.

Preparing for your First Meeting

Before your first official meeting, you will need to gather many documents for the attorney to review. Organize the following documents for your first meeting with the attorney:

- Bank account (checking and saving) statements
- Brokerage account statements
- Mutual fund company statements
- Annuity statements
- IRA and 401(k) statements
- Life insurance policies
- Wills and trusts
- Power of attorney forms
- Tax returns
- Discharge papers
- Marriage certificates
- Business agreements
- Safety deposit box information
- Death certificates
- Real estate deeds

- Mortgage information

- Loans and lines of credit

- Credit card statements

- Information about your children, such as name, address, phone number, and date of birth

Your First Attorney Meeting

After gathering the documents listed you are ready for your first attorney meeting. There are many reasons you would want to meet with an attorney. In most cases, the surviving spouse is named the executor of the estate (discussed in the next section). The attorney can give you guidance as to the best approach to take when you are performing your executor duties. They should be able to save you time by telling you what you do and do not need to do. They may also advise you against doing some things that may cost the estate additional taxes. If the size of your estate and the estate of your deceased spouse is large enough to be subject to estate tax, you will want to be careful before withdrawing any money from your accounts. In some situations, it may be better to disclaim some of the inheritance to reduce the size of your estate (see the discussion "Disclaiming Assets" in Chapter 17, "Tax Issues"). Disclaiming simply means that you are refusing an asset from your spouse's estate and that it should go to the next person in line to receive it. In most cases, this would be your children.

The attorney will also review your deceased spouse's will or trust and determine the correct path to follow. The will should then be filed with the probate court. Most states require that this task be performed within a certain number of days following death. The will also will name the person who will be the executor or personal representative of the estate.

Chapter Fifteen

What Does it Mean to be an Executor/Executrix?

When you are faced with the death of a loved one, it is easy to withdraw and not deal with administrative or clerical issues. However, if you are named as executrix/executor of the estate there are many responsibilities you need to undertake. To simplify, I will use the term executor to apply to either gender.

The executor has a vital role in the administration of the estate. Their main task is to settle and distribute the estate pursuant to the last will and testament. In the simplest form, this requires gathering the assets, paying debts, and distributing the net estate according to the will.

Appointment of Executor

How do you officially become the executor? When you or your attorney file the will with the probate court, the court will issue letters of appointment certifying the authority of the executor. Generally, you should request at least 20 copies of the appointment letter to begin with and go back to the court if you need more. You do not want to have too many, since they normally are required to be recently dated (within the last 60 days). Most institutions that you deal with on behalf of the estate will require this letter before they will work with you on estate issues.

Executor's Duties

The duties of the executor are numerous. While an attorney will take care of some of them, as executor you will need to perform many of them. Remember, the more you do yourself, the less the attorney should charge you. The following are a list of the executor's responsibilities:

- Locate the will and/or trust and other important papers, as stated earlier.

- Hire an attorney to assist with legal matters.

- File with the probate court an inventory of all money and property owned at the date of death.

- Open a bank account in the name of the estate. A separate account should be maintained for all funds of the estate.

- Maintain accurate accounting records in relation to estate assets.

- Notify beneficiaries named in the will.

- Have the value of estate property appraised.

- Notify the post office, creditors, and banks of the individual's death.

- File all required income, inheritance, or estate tax returns.

- File for life insurance, social security, and any employer benefits that may be available or payable to the estate.

- Collect income and amounts due the estate and pay the bills of the estate.

- Consider supervision for decedent's business, or if applicable, complete the sale of the business pursuant to a buy-sell agreement as discussed previously in Chapter 6, "Business Succession Planning," in Part I.

- Manage estate assets and make sure any investments are prudent.

As you can see, a lot of work is involved in being executor of an estate. If possible, you may want other family members to assist you with some of these tasks and lessen your burden. Unless the estate you are dealing with is very simple, it should be clear why you would want to enlist the help of attorneys, accountants, and financial professionals. If you do not want to be the executor, you will need to address the court with this issue. Generally, the will names an alternate choice for the job. If none are named, the court will appoint someone if you do not wish to act in this capacity.

Probate

Probate is a term you hear often, but most people do not understand its meaning. The word "probate" means "to prove." *Black's Law Dictionary* defines probate as "the act or process of proving a will." Probate actually entails the entire estate administration process of determining the decedent's total assets; paying debts, liabilities and taxes; and distributing the remaining estate assets to the proper beneficiaries.

How does probate relate to your situation? It depends on how the decedent's assets were titled. If the decedent had assets in their own name, they will be subject to probate. By having assets "in their own name" I mean assets without beneficiary designations or not held in joint accounts. Assets with beneficiary designations or held jointly will pass automatically to the beneficiary or joint owner and are not subject to probate. Following are examples of nonprobate property:

- Assets owned jointly with right of survivorship
- Bank accounts that utilize pay on death provisions

- Retirement funds with beneficiary designations
- Life insurance with beneficiary designations
- Annuities with beneficiary designations
- Investment accounts that utilize transfer on death provisions

Why do people try to avoid probate? The simple answer is that it can be expensive. The costs include filing fees and attorney fees. As mentioned previously, understanding how you are charged is very important. In some states you can be charged a percent of the estate. This can be very expensive, regardless of how much work needs to be done. The fees can be as high as 5% of the estate. If you have a choice, it is usually best to arrange payment on an hourly basis. If you reside in a state that allows a percent of the estate to be charged, it would probably be best to plan to avoid probate.

It is the executor's duty to inform creditors of his or her appointment by publication and actual notice. Notice by publication requires the executor to publish notice of their appointment in a newspaper of general circulation in the county where the deceased resided. Actual notice should be given to all known creditors. This can be done with a letter. The attorney you work with will often do this for you or will assist you to do it.

After notice has been given, prepare an inventory of assets. The inventory, containing a list of the decedent's assets and their value at the date of death, should be filed with the probate court. Again, this only relates to assets that do not have a beneficiary designation or are not held in a joint account. The inventory you file will become part of the public record and will be available to creditors who may want to pursue the estate for unpaid liabilities.

Tax Issues

There is an old saying, "Nothing in life is sure but death and taxes." When someone does die this old adage sure proves true. Many tax returns may have to be filed, depending on the size of the decedent's estate. If the gross estate is larger than $1,500,000 in 2004, a federal estate tax return needs to be filed. The first $1,500,000 is referred to as the "applicable exclusion amount." The applicable exclusion amount is the amount an individual may leave to their heirs free of tax. The estate may also be subject to a state estate tax. Depending on the state you reside in, a separate filing, which differs from the federal rules, may be required. For example, in Minnesota for 2004, an estate tax return must be filed for estates that are larger than $850,000. The $1,500,000 federal exclusion amount will be changing in the future, as noted in Part I, Chapter 4, "Estate Planning for Married Couples." Other tax returns that need to be filed are federal and state fiduciary income tax returns as well as your regular individual federal and state income tax returns.

Accountants

If the decedent's estate is large enough that an estate tax return is required, you would definitely want to hire a CPA (certified public accountant) who has experience working in this area. In addition, a final individual income tax return for the decedent and an estate income tax return will need to be filed. The final income tax return can be a complicated return because it may contain less than a full year's information. Also, the estate income tax return is subject to complex rules you are probably not familiar with.

You may already have an accountant, but if this person is not a CPA and experienced in this area I would suggest you obtain a referral for a qualified candidate. Call the Society of Certified Public Accountants in your state and obtain names of qualified CPAs. Because a mistake could cost the estate a lot of money, do not try to cut corners in this area. To get a qualified CPA you will pay higher fees than you would to a non-CPA, but it is worth it.

Federal Estate Tax

What is the estate tax? Sometimes called the "death tax," it is simply a tax imposed on wealth transfers made at the owner's death. The tax is assessed on the value of the property being transferred. The individuals or recipients of the estate property do not pay it; the estate pays the tax before the property is distributed.

The estate tax was first imposed in 1797 to pay for a naval buildup in response to heightened tensions with France, and it was abolished just five years later. It was reenacted twice: to pay for the Civil War and the Spanish-American War, and subsequently abolished twice: in 1862 and 1902. Finally, in 1916 it was reintroduced to pay for World War I and has not been repealed since. However, under current law it will be repealed entirely for the year 2010, after which it will return. Between now and 2011, the amount of the applicable exclusion amount changes as follows:

Table 1. Applicable Exclusion Amount

Year	Amount
◆ 2004	$1,500,000
◆ 2005	$1,500,000
◆ 2006	$2,000,000
◆ 2007	$2,000,000
◆ 2008	$2,000,000
◆ 2009	$3,500,000
◆ 2010	Repealed
◆ 2011	$1,000,000

In my opinion, there will be legislation sometime before the 2010 repeal actually happens. I hope this situation will be clarified soon so that individuals can plan appropriately.

Federal Estate Tax Return

If the decedent's gross estate is valued at $1,500,000 or greater in 2004, the estate is required to file a federal estate tax return (Form 706). This is a complicated tax return and *needs to be filed whether or not a tax is due with the return.* An estate valued at less than $1,500,000 is not required to file a return. The return, if required, is due nine months after the date of death. If you need more time to complete the return, you may apply for an extension of time to file that will give you six more months. However, the extension does not extend the period for paying any tax that may be due. Any taxes due must be sent in with the request for an extension.

This return is not like the familiar income tax return. Instead of taxing income, this return taxes the *value* of your assets. So, the question becomes, how do you determine the gross value of the estate? You add up the fair market value of everything the decedent owned and one-half of the fair market value of the assets that were owned jointly. If the value of these items is greater than $1,500,000, an estate tax return will have to be filed. How do you determine the fair market value of the assets? Property such as bank accounts and investment accounts are valued at their fair market value on the date of death. It is a little more difficult when you are valuing real estate such as a home or vacation property. For this reason, I would suggest you hire an appraiser to value the property for you. If the IRS audits the estate tax return, you need to show how you determined the values you used. An appraisal will provide you with solid support for these values. To determine the taxable estate, you are allowed certain deductions for expenses and can subtract any outstanding liabilities of the decedent. There are also marital and charitable deductions, which are discussed in the next paragraphs. Obviously, the tax return is not quite as simple as this, but these items should give you a general idea of some deductions.

Marital Deduction—If you are married, the law allows you some protection. The unlimited marital deduction allows 100% of the property that passes from the deceased spouse to the surviving spouse to escape taxation. This may not be as great an estate planning tool as it sounds, however, because you may just be deferring the tax until the surviving spouse passes away. In this situation, the property received by the surviving spouse may be taxed upon the survivor's death if the surviving spouse's estate is larger than the applicable exclusion amount on the date of death.

The property that qualifies as a marital deduction must be part of the decedent's gross estate. The more common ways for property to pass and qualify for the deduction are as follows:

- under last will and testament
- property owned jointly with right of survivorship

- beneficiary designation (life insurance, IRA, etc.)

This list is not all-inclusive but represents most situations. The marital deduction may be the most important tax savings/deferral tool available to you.

Charitable Contributions—Any charitable bequests made at death through a will or beneficiary designations qualify for a full deduction against the estate. The rules for qualifying the charitable organization are the same as they are for individual income tax charitable deductions. The charity must be an approved nonprofit organization.

Disclaiming Assets

Another important planning tool you should know about if your estate is larger than the applicable exclusion amount, is referred to as a "disclaimer." You may take advantage of this tool for up to nine months after the decedent's passing. To disclaim means to refuse the property that may be left to you. Why would you do this? There are several reasons a person would elect to disclaim assets left to them:

- You may not want the property
- It may increase your estate and create an estate tax problem for you
- Your children may need the assets more than you do

The process to make the disclaimer is complicated and should be done with care. I would suggest that an attorney be involved to make sure all of the proper steps are followed.

To take advantage of the disclaimer provision in the law a number of specific tests must be met.

- Irrevocable and unqualified (once it is agreed to, it is final)

- Written and signed (preferably notarized)

- Timely completion (within nine months of death)

- Correct delivery (proper party must receive the disclaimer)

- No consideration (you may not be paid or benefit by making the disclaimer)

- Cannot accept interest in the property before making the disclaimer (for example, accepting dividends from inherited stock)

If your estate is large enough that it may be subject to estate tax, you most certainly want to determine whether there would be any benefit to disclaiming assets.

Stepped Up/Down Basis

You are probably not familiar with this term, but it could be very valuable to you. A step-up-in-basis means that the basis of an asset is increased to its date of death fair market value as demonstrated in the following examples. Basis is important because it is used to determine your gain or loss on the subsequent sale of property. The step-up basis rule applies to inherited property that can be included in the decedent's gross estate. This applies whether or not a federal estate tax return was filed. The step-up applies to capital gain property (property that would be subject to capital gains tax if sold). It does not apply to assets such as individual retirement accounts (IRAs), annuities, or employer retirement plans (such as a 401(k), profit sharing, pension plans, etc.). A couple of examples follow.

Example: Assume that your deceased spouse owned stock that cost $5,000 on the date of purchase. At the date of death, the value of the stock is $12,000. If the stock is sold before death, there would be a $7,000 capital gain ($12,000 value minus the original cost of $5,000). Let us assume the stock was not sold but still owned at the date of death. Then, the basis of the property receives a basis step-up to the $12,000 fair market value on the date of death. Now if the stock is sold for $12,000 there will be no gain or loss because the basis would also be $12,000.

Example: Now let us assume the deceased spouse had an IRA. The total contributions to the IRA were $4,000. The value at the date of death was $9,000. Because the IRA would not be eligible to be taxed as a capital gain upon distribution, it would not receive a step-up in basis. The $5,000 gain would be taxed as ordinary income when it is distributed.

The basis step-up rule can also become the basis step-down rule as well. If a decedent dies owning property that has declined in value, the basis will be lowered to the date of death value.

What about jointly owned property? The rules also apply, with one exception. The portion of the property owned by the surviving spouse does not receive the step-up.

Example: Assume that you and your deceased spouse jointly own stock that cost $5,000 on the date of purchase. At the date of death, the value of the stock is $12,000. If the stock is sold before death, there would be a $7,000 capital gain ($12,000 value minus the original cost of $5,000). Let us assume the stock was not sold, but was still owned at the date of death. Then the property receives a basis step-up to $8,500. This is computed in the following manner:

½ date of death value *(deceased spouse's step-up)*	*$6,000*
½ of the original basis *(surviving spouse's basis)*	*$2,500*

Now if the stock is sold for $12,000 there will be a gain of $3,500 because the basis of the stock would be $8,500. The stock received a step up in basis equal to one-half of the fair market value that was attributable to the deceased spouse.

Estate Income Tax Returns

The estate, for income tax purposes, is made up of the same assets that are considered probate assets (defined earlier). Income produced by these assets must be reported as income by the estate on Form 1041, U.S. Income Tax Return for Estates and Trusts. The nonprobate assets that pass by law, such as those owned jointly or by beneficiary designation, still have tax-reporting implications, but the reporting is the responsibility of the party who receives the asset. *The executor of the estate must file an estate income tax return if the gross income for the estate is $600 or more.*

In many cases, the estate will distribute income and property to beneficiaries during the period of estate administration. This will have an impact on who will be paying the tax on the income of the estate. For tax purposes, a distribution of cash or property to a beneficiary is generally treated as a distribution of current taxable income.

> *Example: The estate of John Doe has taxable interest income of $2,000 for the current year. During the year, the executor of the estate distributed $3,000 cash to Jane, the sole beneficiary of the estate. In this situation, Jane will be responsible to pay the tax on the $2,000 of taxable interest income because it was distributed to her.*

This does not relieve the estate of filing a tax return for the year. The estate would still file Form 1041, but the return would contain a Schedule K-1, identifying the income that passed to Jane. To simplify, the estate is telling the IRS that Jane received the income and that she is responsible to pay the tax on it.

The first tax year of a decedent's estate begins at the time of the decedent's death. The tax year of the estate must be chosen before the due date of the initial Form 1041. The due date of the return will be the 15th day of the fourth month after the chosen year-end of the estate, which can end in any month you choose since the estate tax year may be less than one year but no longer than 12 months. The tax year must end on the last day of a month. To give you a reference point: think about your personal tax return, Form 1040. This return typically has a year-end of December 31. There may be some tax deferral benefits to the estate by choosing a year-end other than December 31.

> *Example: John Doe died in February 2004. The executor of the estate chose a year-end of January 31. During this tax year, the estate had $40,000 of taxable income. The executor distributed $40,000 of income to Jane Doe in February 2004. The $40,000 income will be reported on the income tax return of the estate for the year ended January 31, 2005. The income will be reported to Jane on a 2004 Schedule K-1. Jane will then report the income on her personal 2005 income tax return, with the tax due on April 15, 2006. Thus the tax is paid 25 months after the distribution was made. This*

allows Jane to defer the tax liability and hold on to her money for a longer period.

This is another example of why it is prudent to work with professionals to settle an estate. Many choices and elections may be made that would benefit the estate if the foresight is available to take advantage of the laws.

If the estate must pay tax on income because distributions are not being made, the estate may have to pay quarterly estimated taxes. Estimated taxes are not required to be paid by an estate until the first tax year ending two or more years after the decedent's death. After that, the executor of an estate is subject to the same estimated tax rules as are individuals. However, no estimated taxes are due if the tax liability of the estate (after credits and backup withholding) is less than $1,000. In addition, no estimated taxes are due if the prior year was a period of 12 months and the estate had no tax liability for that year.

Final Return—Form 1040

When a person dies, income tax returns must still be filed. Death does not excuse tax returns or the payment of taxes. The surviving spouse can still file a joint income tax return in the year in which the spouse's death occurs. The benefit of this is that joint tax rates, which are normally lower, may be used on this final return.

Exemptions, Standard Deductions, and Tax Rates.

Exemptions, standard deductions, and tax rates are not pro-rated in the year of death. For computing income taxes, the decedent is treated as if they were alive for the entire year.

Income and Deductions. The decedent's income and deductions until the date of death are included on the final return. Income earned by the decedent's assets after death is reported on Form 1041, as discussed earlier. As a result, you are breaking the decedent's income tax year into two years and allocating between two types of returns (Form 1040 and Form 1041).

Medical Deductions. The rules for deductions for a decedent are the same as those for individuals. Qualifying expenses paid before death are deductible. However, there is an exception. Medical costs paid from the decedent's estate within one year of the date of death can be deducted on either the decedent's Form 1040, as a deductible expense from the decedent's income, or the estate tax return (Form 706), as a deductible expense from the estate's assets. In many situations, there is no benefit to taking the deduction on the estate tax return, so it often makes sense to take the deduction on Form 1040. To benefit from a deduction on Form 1040, overall medical expenses must be high enough to meet the deductible standard. Medical expenses on a personal return are only deductible to the extent they exceed 7.5% of adjusted gross income. In addition, medical expenses must be deducted in the year the services were provided.

Unrecovered Contract Investments. A little known tax rule may also provide you with some tax relief, especially if your spouse passed away soon after retirement. If the decedent was receiving a pension or annuity before death and the payments were based on their life only, a deduction may be possible for any investment not recovered. The deduction can be claimed as a miscellaneous itemized deduction on Schedule A of Form 1040 and is not subject to the 2% adjusted gross income limitation.

> *Example: John Doe died at age 66. He had purchased an immediate annuity at age 62. An immediate annuity pays a guaranteed monthly amount (based on the insurance company's ability to pay) to the purchaser based on age and current interest rates. John's annuity cost $100,000, which represents John's investment in the contract. The annuity was set up to pay him $500 per month for life. There was no beneficiary named on the annuity, and the payment stream was based on John's life expectancy. It would stop upon John's death. At the time of his death, John had received 45 payments. This totaled $22,500 (45 x $500). Thus, John's loss on the contract would be $77,500 ($100,000–$22,500). This amount is John's unrecovered investment in the contract and may be deducted as a miscellaneous itemized deduction on John's final income tax return.*

> *Example: Joseph Roe retired at age 62. When he retired, he was given three choices as to how he could receive his company pension. The first choice was to*

receive a lump sum distribution of $120,000. The second choice was to receive a payment of $600 per month paid over Joe's life. As a third choice, he could receive a payout of $400 per month based on the life expectancies of both Joe and his spouse. Joe chose the $600 per month option payable over his life. When Joe passed away at age 75 he had received 150 payments, or $90,000 (150 x $600). Because Joe had not received his total investment in the contract, of $120,000, a deduction of $30,000 ($120,000–$90,000) is allowed as a miscellaneous itemized deduction on Joe's final tax return. If Joe had chosen the first or third option, no deduction would be allowed because payments from the contract would continue to be paid to the surviving beneficiary. In this situation, Joe chose the option with no beneficiary, which means that the payments ceased upon his death.

Tax on Sale of Residence

If you sell your principal residence after the death of your spouse, you should be aware of the implications. The tax law allows a married couple to exclude $500,000 of gain on the sale of their principal residence, if they qualify. To qualify for the $500,000 exclusion, you have to have owned the home and used it as a principal residence for at least two out of the five years prior to the sale. The house has to be sold before or in the same year your spouse passed away. If you sell the house in any year following the death of your spouse, you can exclude only $250,000 of gain.

What if you did not live in the house for the required two years? The Internal Revenue Service clarified this question in 2002. If the house was sold after the death of a spouse, but before living in it as a principal residence for two years, the sale would qualify for a partial exclusion.

> *Example:* *John and Jane Doe bought and lived in their house for one year prior to John's death. Jane sold the house six months after John died and purchased a new residence. Normally, any gain would be fully taxable because the home was not used as a principal residence for the required two years. However, under current tax law this would qualify for a partial exclusion. Death is one of the exceptions to the two-year holding period. The exclusion percentage is computed by dividing the number of months the house was owned (18 months) by the required holding period (24 months). The excludable gain would be $187,500 (75% of the normal exclusion of $250,000). The exclusion is only $250,000 because the home was not sold in the year John died.*

Estimated Income Taxes

If you and your spouse had been paying estimated income taxes, you will need to estimate your income for the year following the final tax return. It will most likely be less because of the loss of your deceased spouse's income. Additionally, your filing status will change from married filing jointly to single, unless you still have children at home (which would allow you to file as a qualifying widow). It is important to understand these changes in the first year after a spouse's death.

Applying for Benefits

When a spouse dies, the surviving spouse will generally be entitled to benefits from various sources. You may be eligible for social security benefits, life insurance benefits, veteran benefits, employer benefits, etc. To receive the benefits you are eligible for you will need to apply for them, and the sooner you get started the sooner you will begin to receive your benefits. The following is a brief explanation of the most common benefits and how to apply for them.

Social Security Benefits

Social Security is the benefit most common to widows. No matter what your age, as a widow you may be eligible for Social Security. In most cases, a statement of death is sent to the Social Security office by the funeral home. To initiate a claim, you should call your local Social Security office. To find the telephone number for your local Social Security office, look in the telephone directory under the government section. If you cannot find a local number, you can call 1-800-772-1213. You can also obtain information on the Internet. The Web site address of the Social Security Administration is www.ssa.gov.

Different types of Social Security benefits are available. They include the following:

Death Benefit. You are entitled to a death benefit of $255. This may not be much, but it is better than nothing. A form needs to be completed to obtain the benefit. The funeral director should be able to provide you with the form or might even complete it for you. Or you may obtain the form at your local Social Security office.

Survivor Benefit. There are various types of survivor benefits. The amount of the widow's benefit will depend on the length of time and the amount of Social Security contributions made by the deceased spouse. The deceased must have worked and contributed to the Social Security system for at least 40 quarters. Eligibility for the benefit will vary depending on the situation. First, you qualify if you are younger than age 60 and caring for children. In this situation, you may collect survivor benefits until the youngest child reaches the age of 16. Second, individuals age 50 or older who are disabled are eligible. Third, if you are age 60 or over, you will be eligible to collect the widow's benefits. If you are not yet 65, the benefit is reduced to less than 100%. At age 60, you receive 71.5% of the total benefit. The percent goes up for each year you are closer to age 65.

If you are under age 62 when you begin collecting the widow's benefit, you have the option to collect a benefit based on your own earnings' history upon reaching age 62. If your Social Security benefits are higher than the widow's benefit, it would make sense to choose it instead of the widow's benefit.

Finally, your children can collect benefits at least until they reach age 18. However, if they are still in high school, they may collect through high school graduation or two months after reaching age 19, whichever comes first.

Life Insurance

One of the most important benefits you may be able to collect is life insurance. In many cases, this money will take care of you until you get back on your feet. It also may provide for all or part of your retirement needs. Inform the insurance company of the insured's death. If you are the beneficiary, apply for this benefit as soon as you can.

Life insurance policies will be a company group life policy or a privately purchased policy, or both. If you are the beneficiary of a group policy or some other policy provided by the deceased's employer, you will need to contact the employer's Human Resources department for assistance. They should be able to help you contact the insurance company. If you or your spouse purchased a life insurance policy, you need to look at the policy for an address or a telephone number. You may also want to contact the insurance agent who sold the policy for assistance. However, many times the agent may be retired or no longer in the business because the policy was likely purchased many years before the death occurred. If the agent isn't available, a letter should be drafted and sent to the insurance company informing them of the death. The letter should include the policy number, the insurance policy, and a copy of the death certificate. A sample letter that you can use to inform the insurance company of your spouse's death follows.

Date

Your name
Your address

Insurance Company
Insurance Company's address

Re: Deceased spouse's name
Insurance policy number 00000000

On August 25, 2005, my husband, John Doe, died. I would like to apply for the benefits provided by this policy. I have enclosed a copy of the death certificate and the insurance policy.

continued

> *Please provide me with the forms and instructions I need to apply for the death benefit. I would appreciate it if you could give this matter your prompt attention.*
>
> *If you need to reach me, my telephone number is 333-333-3333.*
>
> *Sincerely,*
>
>
> *Your signature*
> *Your name typed*
>
>
> *Enclosures*

Make a copy of the letter for your file before you mail it. When you mail important papers such as this, use registered mail, with a return receipt requested. In addition, make a copy of the first few pages of the insurance policy that summarizes the benefits of the policy. I suggest this in the unlikely event the policy gets lost in the mail or at the insurance company headquarters. Follow up with a phone call a couple of weeks after mailing your letter if you have not received the forms and information requested from the insurance company.

The insurance company will generally give you three options for receiving your proceeds. The first is a lump sum payment. You will receive a check for the full amount of the policy plus any interest that may have accrued on the policy since death. This option gives you the most flexibility because you can now choose how to use the money. If you choose this option, it would be wise to deposit the money into an interest-bearing account. There is no need to rush into a decision regarding what to do with the money. Wait until you are comfortable. Unless you are a financial professional, it would be wise to work with an advisor on the best course of action to take. (See Part I, Chapter 3, "Choosing a Financial Services Professional.")

The second option is for the insurance company to open an account on your behalf and deposit the death benefit into it. This is usually an interest-bearing account held with the insurance company.

The third option is to choose an annuity. An annuity is a stream of payments for a set amount of time. Generally you would receive a monthly payment for the rest of your life, or another set time period. This option gives you very little flexibility.

I believe the lump sum payment is the best option of the three due to the flexibility it provides. However, there may be times when one of the other options would be appropriate. For example, if the beneficiary has problems controlling spending or does not want to deal with a lump sum amount, you may wish to consider the annuity. If this is the case, I would suggest working with a financial professional to determine if the annuity payout is fair and reasonable.

If you are not sure whether your spouse has a life insurance policy, look through your checkbook for the prior two years to see if any payments were made to an insurance company. Also, call your spouse's employer to ask if your spouse had any life insurance or death benefit coverage. Search your file cabinets and any other place at home where you keep important papers. Check the contents of the safety deposit box. If a policy did exist, in most cases, performing these steps would find it.

Veterans Benefits

If your spouse was a veteran you may be eligible for veterans benefits. If the death is service related, the Veterans Administration will pay a benefit of $2,000. If it was not service related, the amount is limited to $600.

To collect the benefits you need to contact the Veterans Administration. You will need to complete Form 21-530, "Application for Burial Allowance." To obtain the form and instructions needed to complete it, call the Veterans Administration. There is a toll-free number listed in your telephone directory for the Veterans Administration office in your state. They will send you the information necessary to make your claim. Information may also be found on the Internet at www.cem.va.gov.

Employer Benefits

If your spouse was employed at the time of death, benefits are generally available from their employer. The easiest way to find out is to call the Human Resources department of the employer. They should be able to tell you what benefits are available to you. As mentioned earlier, you will want to ask if the company provided life insurance for your spouse and the amount of benefit available to you.

You will likely be entitled to your spouse's final paycheck, as well as any accrued vacation pay. Generally, if your spouse had not taken all of the vacation they were entitled to, you should receive a payment in satisfaction of the unused time. You may also want to find out if the company has a policy of paying employees for unused sick time. If so, you may be entitled to those hours as well.

Retirement Accounts

Usually the most significant benefit may be the decedent's retirement accounts. One of your toughest decisions may be to decide the best way to withdraw the funds. You normally have two choices: taking a lump sum distribution (fully taxable if not rolled over to an IRA account) or annuity payments.

This decision should only be made after analyzing what the best option is for you. To analyze this properly you should have a strong understanding of how annuities work, and this would eliminate most people. I will explain some factors to consider, but I suggest you consult a financial professional with a tax background.

There are numerous variables that come into play when analyzing how to utilize retirement benefits, but I will try to simplify it. If you choose to take a lump sum distribution, the money is yours to invest as you please. This is the easiest piece to understand. However, as discussed later in "Lump Sum Rollovers," a very important decision has to be made on how to roll the money over if you decide to accept a lump sum distribution.

The other option, an annuity, is a stream of payments over a period of time. When dealing with an employer retirement plan, the time period is generally set over the rest of your life. An example of a normal situation considering a lump sum distribution and an annuity option follows.

> *Example: Your spouse's retirement plan has a value of $200,000. You have a choice of receiving a lump sum payment of $200,000 or taking an annuity that would pay you $1,500 per month for the rest of your life (subject to the claims paying ability of the insurance company).*

The question to be answered is which method makes the most sense for you. Many variables come into play when making this decision. Since it is such an important decision, I would advise you to utilize a professional advisor to help you understand the implications. The $1,500 payment may be very good; then again, it is possible that with the $200,000 you could buy an annuity from an insurance company that would pay you $1,700 per month, depending on current interest rates and other variables. On the other hand, you may not want to tie your money up in an annuity and you would like the lump sum.

Annuity Payments

If you decide you want the annuity there will be other decisions regarding guaranteed payout periods. An annuity that pays for the rest of your life could end after one month if you died right away. Therefore, you generally are allowed to choose a period that guarantees payments for the length of the period selected. For example, you may choose to collect payments over the rest of your life, but have a minimum payout period of ten years. This is known as "Life expectancy with a ten-year period certain." In this situation, if you died after six months the annuity payments would continue for the full ten-year period. This allows you to pass the benefit on to your heirs for the specified period. If you live for longer than ten years, the payments will continue until your death. When a period certain is chosen, the monthly amount will be less than it would be when choosing a payout for the rest of your life with no period certain.

Lump Sum Rollovers

If you choose to take the lump sum payment, the amount will need to be moved into a new account. This is known as an IRA rollover that will defer the payment of income taxes until you elect to take distributions. The most common approach is for individuals to roll over the lump sum amount into their own IRA. This is normally the best approach. However, if you have not attained age 59½, you may not want to do this. Once the money is rolled over you cannot access it any longer without incurring a 10% premature distribution penalty until you have attained age 59½. If you are going to need access to the money before age 59½, you should utilize a different strategy.

The investment professional you are using should be able to assist you with this strategy. In this case you will want to set up a beneficial IRA. A beneficial IRA will allow you to access the money in the IRA without incurring the 10% penalty. The account would be titled something like this: National Bank Custodian for Jane Doe as Beneficiary of John Doe. This is an important strategy for widows under age 59½ who need to access IRA money to live on.

Health Insurance

One last employer benefit to explore is health insurance. Having continuing health coverage after your spouse passes away is extremely important. If your spouse worked for a company that employed 20 or more employees, you have the right to continue the health insurance under the federal COBRA law. The company must allow you 60 days to decide whether you would like to continue with your spouse's plan. If you decide to do so, the law provides that you can continue with the existing insurance for 18 months. If you have dependent children, the period could be as long as three years. The premium, which you now have to pay, may seem high, but it is much cheaper than having to buy an individual policy for you or your family.

Chapter Nineteen

Asset Titling and Beneficiaries

After a spouse passes away, any accounts or assets that were titled in or included your spouse's name will need to be changed. This includes beneficiary designations. By now, you have probably made a list all of the accounts you own. If not, you must do this now. Follow the instructions given previously to perform this task.

Whose name should be on the asset? It depends on how the asset was originally titled. If it was a joint account it would be titled in the surviving spouse's name. If the asset was in the decedent's name alone, it will most likely have to be retitled in the name of the estate until the estate is settled, at which time it would again be retitled into the name of the ultimate beneficiary as determined by the will. If a revocable living trust was listed as the owner, it will be retitled in the name of the beneficiary of the trust.

The two most common methods to change title are: (1) writing a letter directly to the institution holding the account, or (2) contacting the person connected to an account, such as an investment adviser. The following sample letter could be used to change the title of an asset that was owned by the decedent and needs to be retitled in the name of the estate.

Date

Your name
Your address

Institution (Bank, Investment Company etc.)
Institution's address

Re: Deceased spouse's name
Account number 00000000

On August 25, 2005, my husband, John Doe, died. I have been appointed personal representative of his estate. I respectfully request that you change the title of the above referenced account to "Estate of John Doe." The ID number of the estate for tax reporting purposes is 41-xxxxxxx.

Enclosed please find a copy of the death certificate and my appointment as personal representative of the estate. I would appreciate it if you would give this matter your prompt attention. If you need to reach me, my telephone number is 333-333-3333.

Sincerely,

Your signature
Your name typed

Enclosures

This letter gives you the basic format to request a title change. It is a good idea to call the institution before sending the letter and inquiring about the institution's rules for title changes. For instance, some institutions may require other documentation to be submitted with the letter. This will help avoid delays resulting from having your request denied for lack of a required document.

The following is a sample letter if the account was held jointly and will be retitled in the surviving spouse's name.

Date

Your name
Your address

Institution (Bank, Investment Company etc.)
Institution's address

Re: Deceased spouse's name
Account number 00000000

On August 25, 2005, my husband, John Doe, died. I have been appointed personal representative of his estate. The above referenced account was a joint account, and I am the joint tenant of this account. I respectfully request that you change the title of the account to Jane Doe. My social security number for tax reporting purposes is 999-99-9999.

continued

Enclosed, please find a copy of the death certificate and my appointment as personal representative of the estate. I would appreciate it if you could give this matter your prompt attention. If you need to reach me, my telephone number is 333-333-3333.

Sincerely,

Your signature
Your name typed

Enclosures

Other assets that need to be retitled, such as real estate, should be done with the assistance of an attorney. If you work with an investment adviser, you can call and tell them of your spouse's death and they should be able to prepare the paperwork to change the titling on the account they handle. Remember to change the titling on all accounts. This also applies to credit cards and other companies or institutions where you do business and pay bills.

Just as important as changing the titles on your assets is changing your beneficiary designations. It is likely that your deceased spouse was the beneficiary on your accounts that have beneficiary designations. Examples of these would be life insurance, IRAs, annuities and transfer-on-death accounts.

In addition, you should have a new will or living trust drafted, which will be discussed later in the book. If you were to pass away it is important that your assets would go to the individuals or charities that you choose.

To change your beneficiary designations, you should contact the institution where the account is held. In most cases, they will have forms that will need to be completed and signed. If you would like, use the previous letter for asset title changes to request beneficiary changes. Revising the letters slightly will do this.

Chapter Twenty

What to Do with Personal Items?

After a spouse dies you are left with many personal items such as clothing, shoes, glasses, sporting equipment, etc. Eventually you will need to deal with these items and decide what to do with them. Everyone will have their own time frame for this. Some individuals prefer to remove items from the house as soon as possible, and others may take a year to accomplish the task. You need to do what makes you comfortable.

In most cases, the best way to take care of personal items is to donate many of them to a local charity. Naturally, you may wish to allow other family members to take items of interest or sentiment to them. There are many charities that will be happy to receive the items that family members do not want. A couple of the more popular charities are Goodwill Industries and the Salvation Army.

The tax savings from making this contribution can be significant, so please do not just box everything up and take it to a local charity. The best approach when donating these items is to first purchase a book titled *It's Deductible: Cash*

For Your Used Clothing. This book will give you all of the guidance you need to make a successful donation. It lists qualified charities and explains the rules that you should follow when making your contribution. In addition, it provides a nice system to record what you are donating, and it also tells you the estimated value of each item contributed.

Generally, when people estimate the value of donated items on their own, they tend to underestimate the value by quite a bit. The workbook sells for approximately $25 and is worth every penny. The workbook is available at Amazon. com or you can call 1-800-976-5358 to order it. If you like to work on a computer, it is also available in a software version.

Chapter Twenty-one

Did Your Spouse Own a Business?

If your spouse owned a business with nonfamily members, hopefully some planning had been completed to address what would happen if one of them passed away. If advanced planning has been completed, it may be as simple as selling your spouse's stock to the other partners under a prearranged plan known as a buy-sell agreement. This agreement generally spells out what will happen with an owner's interest in the business if they pass away. If this is your situation, be thankful. I recommend utilizing the services of a business attorney to assist you with this situation. This will help protect you from those who may want to take advantage of you. As always, be careful when selecting an attorney.

If no buy-sell agreement exists, the situation will be a lot more difficult to resolve. You will need expert advice to navigate you through the negotiations, including an experienced business attorney and a CPA. Most likely, a valuation of the business will need to be completed. Hire an independent valuation specialist to perform this function ve*

for you. Trying to perform these tasks yourself is foolhardy. Depending on the business' value, an error could be a very costly mistake.

If the business is a family business, and you or your children are familiar with it, continuing to operate the business may be a wise choice. If no one wants the business or is familiar with it, consider having the business appraised and selling it. There are many variables in this situation that can be discussed among family members when deciding what to do. If you decide to sell, once again find professionals to assist you.

170

Chapter Twenty-two

Major Decisions

One bit of advice that I strongly recommend you follow is not to make major decisions in the first six months after your spouse's death. In some cases do not make them for a year. This does not mean you should delay everyday decisions. But major decisions, such as selling your home or investing a large insurance settlement, should be postponed.

After such a significant loss, the bereaved one often finds it hard to focus and make good decisions. In such a state it would be easy to decide an issue based on emotions and not see or consider all of the related issues. As time passes, these decisions will be easier and you will be more comfortable making decisions.

My mother lost her second husband in 2002, and initially felt she wanted to sell her house and move into an apartment. I urged her to stay in the house for one year. After that time period if she still wanted to move, I said I would support her decision. Well, after about six months, she decided that she was comfortable in the house and wanted to stay there. The issues that initially concerned her, such as house maintenance and yard work, never became problems because family members helped her out. If she would have moved and not been happy, the situation would have been hard to undo, and she would have suffered more.

If you have been working with a financial advisor over the years and have a trusted relationship, it is okay to continue as you have in the past. However, a new financial advisor coming into your life raises some concerns. If you do not know this person, you may not be in the proper state of mind to determine if you can trust this individual. Therefore, if you do not have an established relationship I recommend keeping your money in an interest-bearing account. This is not the time to take on a lot of risk. Wait until you feel more comfortable with your new advisor before moving forward. (Refer to Part I, Chapter 3 for advice about finding and interviewing a financial professional.)

Chapter Twenty-three

Looking to the Future

Congratulations. You have accomplished a lot to get to this point after the death of your spouse. It is not easy to have to deal with all of these issues while you are grieving, but life does not give you a choice.

Now it is time to begin planning for the next phase of your life. Part III of this book will detail how to properly structure your financial and estate plan to meet your ongoing needs and make it easier for your heirs when you pass away.

Part Three

A New Life

Be not afraid of life.
Believe that life is worth living,
and your belief will create the fact.

—Henry James

Now it begins, the first day of the rest of your new life. As you surely know by now, life is no longer going to be the same as it was. Activities you participated in with your spouse, you now will encounter on your own. You have no doubt continued with some of these activities, but more than likely you are beginning to explore new interests, or at least are thinking about it. You are continuing relationships with some of your old friends and perhaps making new ones.

You have likely come to the understanding that you have a choice to make at this point. You can seclude yourself and withdraw from life, or you can meet it head on and get involved. Part I of this book covered how important it is to be involved in social activities. I hope that you have a strong circle of support from your friends and family. If so, keeping active will not be a problem. If not, you will need to reach out more. The people who survive and flourish are the ones who take the attitude that they are going to make the most out of the rest of their lives. I hope you can embrace this spirit and thrive!

Many issues in Part I of this book are written in relation to married couples. However, many of these issues are still pertinent to you as a single person. I will revisit these areas and point out how they may need to be adjusted because you are now single. In addition, many other issues that relate to widows will be addressed in Part III. One thing to remember: planning is important at any stage in life, but the planning you do from here on may be the most important of your life. The possibility of a second marriage—yes, it could happen—can introduce extra complications into your situation. In addition, the estate planning you do this time may be the last that you do. With that in mind, let us continue.

Chapter Twenty-four

Housing

Since you lost your spouse, your current housing may or may not be suitable for you. As emphasized in Part II, in most situations you should defer your decision for one year. My mother originally intended to sell her house soon after her husband passed away, but after six months she realized the house still met her needs quite nicely. And, in most cases, your home holds many good memories that can provide you with a level of comfort. You are already familiar with the neighbors, the neighborhood, and local shopping and services. After suffering the loss of a spouse, it is difficult to have to adjust to a completely new style of living, let alone a new residence and neighborhood.

A major issue that may have an impact on whether to keep your house is maintenance. Who will mow the lawn, shovel the sidewalk, rake the leaves, or fix the many little problems that can come up? If you have children living nearby, they might assist with these chores. Many times there are kids in the neighborhood who would like to earn some money and will help you. Maybe the neighbors themselves would be glad to pitch in to keep you as a neighbor. Some maintenance chores may be done by community organizations that provide volunteers to assist people who are unable to perform these tasks. Another good option, if you can afford it, is businesses that offer these services. Whatever you do, however, do not hire the two fellows in the next story...

Two not-so-bright guys drove their truck into a lumberyard to pick up some wood. One of them went into the store and told the clerk he needed some four-by-twos. The clerk corrected him and said, "You mean two-by-fours, don't you?" The fellow said, "Just wait one minute and I'll check." With that, he ran out to the truck and returned shortly. He said, "You are right, two-by-fours is what I need." The clerk said, "Ok, how long do you need them?" The fellow once again said, "I'll go check." This time it took him much longer to return and when he did, he said, "We're going to need them a long time. We're building a house."

All jokes aside, good-quality businesses and service people are capable of providing the home maintenance that will allow you to stay in your home. Talk to your friends, family, and neighbors to get referrals for reliable maintenance service businesses.

Home Safety and Security

If none of the above resources are available, you may have no choice but to look at alternative housing. However, if you determine you can and do want to stay in your home, you may want to make some changes to make it safer and more secure. Consider the following, if you do not already have them:

- Install motion-detector lights on your outside entrances. These lights will come on automatically as someone approaches your door.

- Make sure your home has adequate inside lighting. Use higher wattage bulbs and install night-lights in your hallways and/or bathrooms.

- Install a phone in your bedroom so it is more accessible in emergencies.

- Install grab bars by your bathing facilities and toilet to help prevent falls.

- Consider installing a security system. Studies show that if a would-be criminal approaches your house and realizes it is protected with a security system, the criminal will more often than not move on to a house that is not protected. I would suggest you purchase one from a store and not use the type in the following joke...

A burglar broke into a house one night because he knew the residents were out for the night. He was walking through the living room when he heard a voice say, "Jesus is watching you." This froze him in his tracks. He didn't hear anything more and started walking again only to hear the voice again say, "Jesus is watching you." He stopped again and was very frightened. He began to look around, and he spotted a parrot cage in the corner. He asked the parrot, "Was that you that said Jesus is watching?" The parrot said "Yes," and the burglar breathed a sigh of relief. "What's your name?" the burglar asked the parrot. The parrot replied "Clarence." "That's a dumb name for a parrot," said the burglar. "What fool named you that?" The parrot replied, "The same fool that named the Doberman pinscher Jesus."

Many other modifications can be made to make your home safer and friendlier as you grow older. Nevertheless, the items listed earlier should definitely be some of the first changes you consider.

Financial Benefits

Keeping your home can also offer some financial benefits. If you need cash over short periods, you may want to utilize a home equity loan. The interest on such a loan is tax deductible, and the interest rate is generally lower. Remember, though, as discussed in Part I, if you cannot repay the loan, you are putting your home at risk.

If you do not have a lot of money and your net worth is tied up in your home, consider a reverse mortgage. A reverse mortgage is generally more expensive than are traditional loans. While a reverse mortgage is a good option for those who need the income and have no other sources, I believe this should be used as a last resort when seeking additional income.

Reverse Mortgage

To qualify for a reverse mortgage you must be 62 years of age and be using the house as your personal residence. Any outstanding loan against the house must be paid off at closing. A reverse mortgage will give you the choice of taking the proceeds as a lump sum of cash, monthly payments, a line of credit, or as a combination of these options. The money you receive is tax-free. There are formulas in place that limit how much equity you can take out of your home. You can never owe more than what your home is worth at the time of repayment. For example, if you are taking a monthly income and live until age 110, you could theoretically receive more in payments than the house is worth. Instead, your repayments would be limited to the value of the house or the outstanding balance of your reverse mortgage loan, whichever is lower. The loan must be repaid when you die, sell the home, or permanently move out of the home.

Is a reverse mortgage right for you? Before you decide, consider all your options. You may qualify for other, less costly credit plans. Information to help you decide is available from the following sources:

AARP
601 E Street NW
Washington, DC 20049
1-800-424-3410
www.aarp.org/revmort

The National Center for Home Equity Conversion
360 N. Robert Street, #403
St. Paul, MN 55101
1-651-222-6775
www.reverse.org

U.S. Department of Housing and Urban Development (HUD)
451 7th Street SW
Washington, DC 20410
1-888-466-3487
www.hud.gov/offices/hsg/sfh/hecm/rmtopten.cfm

HUD also can refer you to a HUD-approved reverse mortgage counselor. Call HUD toll-free at 1-888-466-3487 or 1-800-569-4287.

Federal Trade Commission
Consumer Response Center
600 Pennsylvania Avenue NW
Washington, DC 20580
www.ftc.gov
1-877-FTC-HELP (1-877-382-4357)

Alternative Housing

What if you decide that staying in your house will not work? There are many possibilities other than a single-family home. You may want to consider an apartment, town home, or condominium. Another area to look at is housing targeted towards seniors, such as independent senior housing, assisted living residences, or a continued care retirement community.

These are all good options, and this list is not all-inclusive. A major advantage to these forms of housing is that they offer maintenance-free living. This can take a lot of worry and stress out of your life. You should get together with family members, visit the various housing options available in your community, and see what is right for you. The following should give you a little better idea about each of the options listed.

Apartment. An apartment is a room or suite of rooms designed as a residence and generally located in a building occupied by several households. You do not own any part of the building or the land. For the right to live on the premises, you pay rent monthly, which covers the maintenance and upkeep of the building and property, and may include some utilities.

Condominium. A condominium is similar to an apartment, but you own it. Essentially, you own the space from the paint on the walls on in. This is considered your exclusive real estate. There are also common elements such as the land the building is built on, the hallways, amenities, etc. You own an interest in these areas, but not one particular physical part. There are also limited common elements such as balconies, parking spaces in an underground garage, etc., which are exclusively for your use, but are still considered common property. You have to pay monthly association dues to pay for the ongoing expenses and maintenance of the building complex, including snow removal and lawn care.

Assisted Living. Assisted living bridges the gap between living on your own and living in a nursing home. Assistance with daily living activities such as bathing, dressing, eating, housekeeping, and transportation is provided. The assistance needed may not require round-the-clock skilled health care that a nursing home provides, yet the individual in this environment has needs that cannot be met living in a more independent setting. Choices will vary from single or double rooms to suites and apartments. In some areas of the country, assisted living residences may be called different names, such as personal care, residential care, or domiciliary care. Assisted living residences may be part of a retirement community, nursing home or elderly housing facility, or they may be stand-alone facilities. Whatever the setting, assisted living offers residents the opportunity to continue living as independently as possible. Costs in assisted living residences range from less than $1,800 a month to $3,200 or more a month, depending on the services and accommodations offered. The facility's charges will reflect the number of services to which you have access. In addition to basic charges, there may be extra charges for some services. The cost may also vary according to the size of the room or apartment.

Independent Living Communities. Often referred to as "retirement communities" or "senior apartments." Independent living communities are designed for seniors who are able to live on their own, but desire the security and conveniences of community living. Some Independent living communities offer recreational activities, which may include swimming pool/spas, exercise facilities, general stores, beauty shops, lounges, libraries, etc. Some may also provide laundry facilities, linen service, meals or access to meals, local transportation, and planned social activities. Health care is not provided with your normal fees, but many communities will allow residents to pay for a home health aide or nurse to come into their apartment to assist with medicine and personal care. Depending on location, amount of living space, and style of the buildings, you can expect the cost to be in the range of other (nonsenior) rental prices in your area. Units are usually rented monthly, and tend to cost less than other types of senior housing. Cooperatives, where residents own their units, are becoming popular in some areas. Since no health care is provided, senior apartment rents aren't covered by Medicare, Medicaid, or long-term care insurance. A subsidized complex may charge on a sliding scale.

Continuing Care Retirement Community (CCRC). The CCRC is known in some regions as a Life Care Community. Religious organizations, fraternal groups, and other nonprofit agencies sponsor most CCRCs. These communities provide comprehensive residential and health care services. This type of community is different from other housing and care options for older people because it offers a long-term contract, which provides for housing, services, and nursing care, usually all in one location. The CCRC continues to meet residents' needs as they grow older in a familiar setting. A CCRC resident can take advantage of a wide variety of activities and services conveniently offered within the community.

An Opportunity to Clean Out the Old

If you decide to move out of your house, you will have the opportunity to clean out many of the items that you have accumulated over the years. We all keep things we do not need and we hate to move them. What is the best way to get rid of this stuff? I can think of four ways. First, you can give items to friends and family. But even they would not want everything. Second, you can make a noncash charitable contribution to charity. There are organizations such as Salvation Army and Goodwill Industries that will accept these noncash items. You will receive a deduction on your tax return and be relieved of the headache of having a garage sale. For a more in-depth discussion, see Chapter 20, "What to do with Personal Items" in Part II. If you cannot itemize your deductions on your tax return and you use the standard deduction allowed by the Internal Revenue Service, then you should use the third option: have a garage sale and let your neighbors and community bargain hunters buy your goods. The fourth option is to let the garbage haulers take it away.

Financial Issues

Now that you are on your own, you must deal with financial issues. Not only will you have to budget your money and pay bills, you will need to decide how to handle your investments. Some people have very little experience with these issues because their spouse performed them. Even if you use a financial professional, the information in this chapter will be helpful and informative. This section of the book gives you the basics so you can get started, if you haven't already.

Will My Money Last?

A major concern for new widows is whether the money they have will support them for the rest of their lives. This question can be looked at two ways: resources and spending. *Resources* are savings accounts and other investments that are available, along with Social Security and pensions. Are they enough to provide a level of income sufficient to support you in the lifestyle you are accustomed to? I hope so, but unfortunately, that is not always the case. If the answer is no, then *spending* will need to be controlled to a level of living less than you are accustomed to, unless your resources can be increased. Once you are retired, it is very difficult to obtain additional resources, so let's focus on spending.

In most cases, people do not know how much money they are spending. You can use the budgeting section that follows to get an idea of what your monthly spending needs are. I suggest you complete the worksheet after reading this section and learn whether you are spending more than you are receiving on a monthly basis. If this is the case, a strategy needs to be identified to make up for the shortfall. As you can see in the worksheet, interest and dividends are included as an income source. However, I generally find that people do not include these amounts as a cash flow source if they are not currently spending their interest and dividends. They reinvest these earnings back into the account and consider them part of their principal. Instead, the reinvested interest and dividends should be included as a cash flow source.

A rule of thumb I use when determining how much of a portfolio you may be able to spend without invading the principal is to withdraw no more than 5% per year. This is based on the belief that between investments in stocks, bonds, and cash a 5% earnings rate is a safe assumption. But with interest rates at an all-time low and much uncertainty in the stock and bond markets, this now seems a bit aggressive. There is never a guarantee, but a more conservative approach would be to use 4% when estimating how much you could withdraw from a portfolio without reducing the principal. In reality, how much you can withdraw will be dictated by the performance of your underlying investments.

In your situation, you know how much interest and dividends you are earning. When you complete the budget worksheet you will include these amounts in your calculation. The only remaining question is whether you should include any of the growth in your other investments such as stocks and real estate. If you do, I would again be conservative and not use more than 5%. For example, if you have $100,000 in stocks, you might assume an extra $5,000 per year as a resource. If after completing the budget worksheet you do not have enough income to cover your spending needs, there are two more options. First, you could spend some of your principal. You may want to consider speaking with a financial advisor about purchasing an immediate annuity that will pay you a stream of income for a period of time (determined by you). This could be for a certain number of years or for your lifetime. When you purchase an annuity, you give the insurance company a sum of money and, in return, they promise to pay you a stream of income for the period determined by you. The payment stream you receive is calculated based on current interest rates and the payout period you select. You must remember that when you pass away the annuity will stop and your investment will be gone, unless you choose a "period certain" as part of your payout option (see the section titled "Annuity Payments" in Chapter 18, "Applying for Benefits," in Part II).

An annuity can increase your monthly cash flow, because it is using your principal in addition to the earnings. This strategy is becoming more common as more companies use alternative retirement plans, such as 401(k) plans instead of traditional pensions, that pay an individual an income for as long as they live. Thus, an immediate annuity can be a viable option when structuring cash flows in retirement.

Last, if you do not want to spend your principal, you will need to reduce your spending. For most people, this is not enjoyable, but it is possible. It is not enjoyable because when you cut spending, you always cut out the fun stuff like vacations and entertainment but must continue to pay the utilities. For ideas on how to spend less, see the section of this chapter titled "How to Spend Less."

Budgeting

Do you run out of money some months? Or does a large balance build up in your checking account over time? How can you control this? The answer is by budgeting.

A budget is a tool to help control and plan your finances; it is an itemized forecast of an individual's income and expenses expected for some period in the future. Unless you understand what and where your money comes from and goes to you will have difficulty being successful with it. If you are running out of money, you are spending more than you can afford. If your checkbook balance is growing, this is a sign you may not be putting your money to work for you.

The first step to controlling your finances is setting up a budget. If you do not know how much you spend, you cannot control it. It does not hurt to be frugal, but try not to be as frugal as Shorty and Mary are in the following joke:

Shorty and Mary went to the state fair every year. Each year when they arrived, Shorty would see the airplane ride and say to Mary that he wanted to take a ride on it. "Well, Shorty," Mary would say every year, "That ride costs $10, and you know $10 is $10." As a result each year Shorty would not get to ride the airplane.

Well, this year Shorty and Mary arrived at the state fair for their 51st year in a row. When they arrived Shorty turned to Mary and said, "Mary, I am 71 years old, and if I don't ride the airplane pretty soon, I will never get to ride it." Mary predictably replied, "Shorty, the ride costs $10, and you know $10 is $10."

The operator of the airplane ride overheard the conversation and approached Shorty and Mary. He said, "I've got a deal for you, I will let you ride for free *under one condition. No one can make a noise during the entire ride or you have to pay the $10." Shorty and Mary agreed to this and got on the ride. The operator of the ride was giving them the ride of their life and trying to scare them into making a noise. He made the ride go really fast and upside down, but no matter what he tried they did not make a sound. Finally the ride was over, and the operator walked up to Shorty and said, "I'm impressed, I gave you the scariest ride I could, and neither of you made a sound."*

Shorty replied, "Yeah, it was hard. I almost said something when Mary fell out, but you know $10 is $10."

It's obvious that Shorty and Mary count their pennies, but then again so do many rich people. You might have had an idea of how much you were spending when your spouse was alive, but now things have changed. Your expenses are most likely less now than before, but in all likelihood so is your income. The key to successful budgeting is being able to identify where you are spending your money and analyzing it. Your income should be easy to track. It most likely comes from the same sources each month, like Social Security, pension, investments, etc. When people have problems with their budget the answer usually lies in reducing spending and not increasing income, because the income is usually fixed and the individual has no ability to increase it.

To make it easier for you to track your income and spending I have included a worksheet for you to use. To complete the monthly budget amount column on the spreadsheet you are going to need to do some work. For each expense that applies, look back through your checkbook to find the average amount you have been spending. For example, if your utility bills for the last six months have been $100, $120, $140, $90, $80 and $130, the average is $110 per month ($660 divided by 6 months). Now do this for all of your other expenses. After you have identified what you have been spending, it is time to complete the budgeted amount column of the worksheet. Many expenses such as utilities and insurance will be the same as the averages you have computed. These are fixed expenses and not likely to change. If a category does not exist in the worksheet for your income or expense, create another row. When you prepare a budget, the variable expenses such as entertainment and eating out are the expenses that may be reduced. These expenses are discretionary and you can control them. For example, you can control how much you eat out by having more meals at home. The amounts you enter as budgeted should be your goal for the amount you spend on these items each month. The lower you keep your expenses, the better your cash flow will be.

An Act of Love

Figure 5. Budget Worksheet

Category	Monthly Budget Amount	Monthly Actual Amount	Differenc
Income:			
Wages			
Interest income			
Social Security			
Pension income			
Dividend income			
Miscellaneous income			
Average annual stock growth–5% (multiply your stock holdings by 5%)			
Income subtotal			
Expenses:			
Mortgage or rent			
Utilities: gas/water/electric/trash			
Cable TV			
Telephone			
Home repairs/maintenance			
Car payments			
Gasoline/oil			
Auto repairs/maintenance/fees			
Other transportation (tolls, bus, subway, etc.)			
Child care			
Auto insurance			
Home owners/renters insurance			
Computer expense			

Entertainment/recreation			
Groceries			
Toiletries, household products			
Clothing			
Eating out			
Gifts/donations			
Health care (medical/dental/ insurance)			
Hobbies			
Interest expense (Credit cards, fees, loans other than mortgages)			
Magazines/newspapers			
Federal income tax			
State income tax			
Social Security/Medicare tax			
Personal property tax			
Pets			
Miscellaneous expenses			
Expenses Subtotal			
Cash Flow (income less expenses)			

I hope that after completing the budget worksheet that you will show a positive, not a negative, cash flow. Once you know how much extra cash you may have on a monthly basis, you can set up a savings plan to put the extra money to work for you. Generally, it is not wise to leave excess cash in your checkbook because checking accounts pay no or very low interest, and when money is left in a checkbook it is more likely to get spent.

If you have a negative cash flow (more expenses than income), you will need to review your budgeted amounts and see if there are any expenses that can be reduced.

Now that your budget is set up or revised, you can use this form each month. Complete your actual monthly expenditure column and see how it compares to the budgeted amounts. This will tell you if your budgeted amounts are wrong and need to be adjusted or if you are spending more than you budgeted. In my experience, the overspending occurs in the fun areas such as vacations, new cars, eating out, gifts, and miscellaneous expenses. As mentioned earlier, fixed costs are hard to reduce, but the variable expenses are discretionary and allow for the most adjustment.

How to Spend Less

I see a lot of people who live beyond their means by choice. They will buy a house or car that is much nicer than their budget really can support. Once they buy these items, they are stuck with the payments for many years to come. Today, it almost seems to me like this is an epidemic in America. According to the United States Federal Reserve, the amount of personal debt held by Americans has doubled in the last ten years. It is easy to be caught up in this madness because our society encourages it. Everything is easy to buy with no money down and affordable payments. However, many people soon have so many affordable payments that they can no longer afford them. Do not try to compete with your friends and neighbors to have the next "best thing." In most cases, you don't need it.

Controlling expenses can be very challenging. The ways to spend more money are trumpeted, but you hear very little on how to spend less. The following is a list of some possible ways to save money and spend less.

- Don't buy anything while waiting in the checkout line at the grocery store.
- Before you purchase it, always ask yourself if you need it.
- Buy items when they are on sale.
- Use coupons.
- Reduce the number of times you eat out by one-half.
- Frequent restaurants with reasonable prices; avoid the expensive establishments.

- Set up an automatic savings plan; when it is deducted from your checkbook you will get used to living without it.

- Refinance your mortgage to ensure you're paying the lowest interest rate.

- Stop smoking.

- Buy generic brands.

- Avoid using credit cards.

- Establish a hobby that allows you to earn money.

- Shop for lower home and auto insurance rates.

- Shop for lower telephone rates; call and ask your current carrier what type of "deals" are available.

- When buying electronics, do not buy the newest technology; prices always come down within a couple of years.

- Do not leave large balances in your checkbook.

- Use the public library instead of buying books.

- Drive used cars.

- Take care of yourself to reduce future health costs.

- Maintain the proper amounts of life, health, and property insurance.

- Prepay your mortgage or other debt whenever you can.

- If employed, contribute to a retirement plan to obtain your employer's matching contribution.

- Lower your cable or satellite television viewing bills by canceling premium channels.

- Cancel magazine subscriptions if you are not reading the magazines.

- Shop on the Internet to find lower prices, but remember to take shipping and handling charges into account.

This list is not all-inclusive, but you get the idea. Cut where you can. I always think about how thrifty my mom can be. She came from a generation that knew how to save and get by on less. She has taught me not to waste and to make good use of what I have. Everyone would benefit from doing more of this.

Cash Flow Planning

A question I'm asked quite often is, "Which of my accounts should I withdraw my living expenses from?" In other words, if you have retirement accounts that hold tax-deferred money and investment accounts that hold after-tax dollars, from which one should you withdraw your needed funds? The answer revolves around income taxes.

Let me illustrate this for you in the way of an example. Let's say an individual would like to retire this year at the age of 60. Over the last few years, this person has deposited approximately $150,000 into a money market account, and is not eligible for Social Security until age 62. Annual living expenses are $40,000. This individual also has a large amount of money in their IRA account and some other nontaxable accounts.

The first reaction for most people would be to use the money in the money market account. What they see is that the money market account would be large enough to pay the bills until the individual could begin collecting their Social Security. In addition, because the money consists of after-tax dollars, they will have to pay no income taxes. Why pay taxes before you have to? What a great scenario!

Not so fast. Tax-bracket planning is discussed in Chapter 27, "Income Taxes," and that is what comes into play here. In this example, the person may be paying no income taxes, but they are also wasting the low tax brackets. In our tax system, we have a 10% and a 15% tax bracket in addition to many others. I always advise people to use these brackets because some day it is likely that they or their children will pay tax on their money in a higher bracket. What does "use these brackets" mean? It means that in this and other examples individuals should generate taxable income and pay tax at these low rates. How do you generate income? Very simple: take a distribution from your IRA or annuity.

When trying to decide which account to withdraw from, it is ideal if you have both tax-deferred and after-tax accounts. Generally, I advise that you take some from each account to manage your tax bracket. You should withdraw just enough from your IRA to keep yourself within a certain tax bracket. For many people, this may be a 15% bracket, but depending on how much money you have, it could be a higher bracket. Some people will withdraw just enough to keep their Social Security from being taxed (discussed in the "Taxation of Social Security Benefits" section of Chapter 27, "Income Taxes").

If you withdraw your money wisely, you can possibly extend the life of your investment accounts by reducing the amount of income tax you pay. Can you figure this out on your own? Not likely. I don't believe most individuals have the skills or the software to analyze this. So, in most cases, it is wise to work with someone who has both an investment and a tax background to assist you with this type of planning.

Bill Paying

Bill paying sounds like a simple task, and it is if you are organized and have a system. I believe being disorganized is the most common reason bills are not paid. Certainly another reason may be lack of money, but that is beyond the scope of this discussion. There are certain unwritten rules when it comes to paying bills and if you follow them bill paying will not take that much time or be a dreadful chore. If you did not read Chapter 1, "Record Keeping" in Part I of this book, now would be a good time to do so. Some of that material is repeated here for emphasis.

The first rule is to find a spot that works well for paying your bills, like an office or a room with a table or desk where you can work. Once you find your spot, always pay your bills there. Preferably, this will be the location where you can keep your records as well. The more you can keep things together the better.

Generally, your bills will be due twice a month, on the 1st and the 15th. Pay your bills on the same days each month if possible, making it routine. Pick days like the 10th and the 24th of the month to be your regular bill-paying days.

Each month as your new bills come in the mail, put them in a file folder titled "Current Bills." When it is your day to pay bills, sit down in your work area and get out your current bill file. As you write out your checks to pay your bills, record the amounts in your checkbook. Also, write on each receipt the check number and the date the bill was paid; this may save you time later. After the check and remittance form is ready to mail, file your receipts as detailed in Chapter 1.

If you would like to make the bill-paying process easier yet, use an automatic payment program. Most companies or organizations to which you owe money will have an automatic payment plan. Look at your bills the next time you pay them. There will probably be an offer for this feature somewhere on the bill or accompanying information. The company will have you sign an agreement giving them the right to withdraw the amount due from your bank account on a certain day each month. The process has actually been around a long time and works quite well.

There are many advantages of using automatic bill paying. Your postage will be reduced. Late payments are no longer a problem, which in turn helps protect your credit rating. Some companies, like an insurance company, will not add an extra monthly charge if you pay your property insurance monthly instead of all at once. You will still have to pay some of your bills with a check, but this process will allow you to simplify your bill paying quite a bit.

One last possibility to consider is online banking. If your bank or credit union supports a software program such as Quicken, QuickBooks, Microsoft Money, or Managing Your Money, or offers its own software (usually free), you can store financial data on your computer and transfer information between your computer and your bank's computer. Using your financial management program or bank-supplied software, you can maintain your records, view the latest information about your accounts, and have the bank write checks from your accounts to pay bills.

Records Retention

Another question I hear quite often is "How long should I keep my records?" The answer is "It depends." The following table should give you guidance as to how long you should keep various types of records.

Table 2. Records Retention

Cancelled checks	3 years
Bank deposit slips	3 years
Bank statements	6 years
Brokerage statements	Until you sell the securities purchased
Retirement plan statements	Keep your annual summaries until you close the account. Keep quarterly reports for one year.
Supporting documents for tax returns	7 years
Tax returns	Permanently
Real estate records	Permanently
Bills/receipts	Three years, except for major purchases and home and car repairs (retain as long you still have the item purchased)

Credit Cards and Debt

If you have credit cards, be careful how you use them. In my opinion, if you cannot pay the bill off each month, do not use the card. A credit card can be a very convenient tool for making purchases. However, it also makes it easy to spend money. You may not make as many purchases if you had to write a check. Before you buy the item, ask yourself if you would be buying it if you had to write a check. If the answer is no, don't buy the item. If possible, you never want to carry an unpaid balance on your credit card because the interest rates are typically much higher than other forms of credit.

If you are currently carrying a balance on your credit card, devise a plan to pay it off. If possible, pay an extra amount each month to reduce the balance. If you can pay extra each month, direct those payments to the balance due on the credit card that charges the highest interest rate. When that balance is paid off, direct your payments to the credit card with the next highest interest rate. If you are regularly saving money, it may make sense to stop saving a monthly amount and redirect those funds to the credit card payments until they are paid off, and then resume your savings plan. You may want to call the credit card company and ask if they will reduce the rate they are charging you. Do not be surprised if they work with you and reduce the rate. I have seen it happen.

Sometimes it might be worthwhile to transfer the balance on your credit card to a lower interest rate credit card. Most people get offers in the mail weekly. If you do make such a transfer, understand for what period the new lower interest rate is effective. Generally, credit card companies will keep the rate down for six months to a year. Hopefully, you will be able to pay off the balance in that time. Another possibility would be to consolidate your loans and credit card balances into one new loan with a lower interest rate. Many times people will do this with a home equity loan. You must remember that using a home equity loan does put your house at risk if you cannot repay the loan. Under no circumstances should you use your credit cards any longer if you have been in trouble once. The likelihood is that you will do so again.

Mortgages

Should I be prepaying my mortgage? This is another question I hear quite often. The answer, once again, is not clear-cut. Many variables come into play, such as interest rates, taxes, emotions, etc. In some situations, the decision is easy because certain individuals do not like debt and want to pay it off as fast as possible. If you are like this, I would suggest you prepay your mortgage because you will sleep better at night and your comfort is what is most important.

What about people who just look at it as a financial issue? Many people say that if you can earn a better return in the stock market than the rate of interest you have on your mortgage, you should not prepay the mortgage. For example, if your mortgage rate is 6%, these people will tell you that the long-term return on stock investments is 10% or 11%, and thus the stock market would be a better place for your money. I have a problem with this. I do not think they are comparing apples with apples. Why? Because, a 6% mortgage does not carry the same risk that the stock market does. When you pay off a mortgage you know the return is 6%. If you put money in the stock market, there is a risk that you could lose your money. I believe if you are deciding whether to prepay your mortgage or invest your money elsewhere, you should look at what the return would be on a more conservative investment like a ten-year corporate bond. For example, if a ten-year corporate bond was paying 7% and your mortgage was 6% I would not advise prepaying the mortgage. If the ten-year corporate bond paid 5%, I would prepay the mortgage. Many times when you hear this topic discussed, the tax deductibility of mortgage interest is brought up. While this is a consideration, you have to also consider that the interest earned on the ten-year corporate bond is also subject to tax. In this situation, it makes more sense to compare the before-tax percentage rates because you will come to the same conclusion whether you compare before- or after-tax percentages. The only time it will make sense to consider after-tax percentages is when your conservative investment is a tax-exempt investment like a government or municipal bond, which may not be subject to federal or state income taxes.

Example: *Your mortgage rate is 6% and you are using a municipal bond issued by your state of residence for your alternative investment. The earnings on the municipal bond are not subject to income tax. Let us assume that your combined federal and state income tax rate is 30%. This is composed of a 25% federal rate and a 5% state rate. Your bond is paying 3.5% interest that will not be subject to the 30% federal and state tax. Your after-tax equivalent earnings rate on the bond would be 5%. This is computed by dividing the 3.5% rate of return by 1 minus the tax rate you are saving (3.50 / .70). The after tax rate of interest you are paying on your loan is 4.2%. This is computed by multiplying your 6% interest rate by 1 minus the applicable tax rate (6.00 x .70). In this situation, you are earning more interest (5%) on an after-tax basis than you are paying on your mortgage (4.2%). Economically, prepaying the mortgage does not make sense.*

Chapter Twenty-six

Investments

This is one of the most important areas relating to financial life. Your investments represent, in most cases, the quality of life that you may be able to maintain. Caution and prudence are of the utmost importance. Frequently I see magazines or newspaper columns giving advice on how to handle your own investments and how easy it is. My belief is that if you do not have a lot of experience in this area, you should not do it by yourself. During the 1980s and 1990s, the stock market went up and up. In most cases I witnessed, if you bought U.S. stocks and bonds, everything went up and you looked like a genius, at least for a while. In 2000, we began to see a change. The markets started going down and the gains began to disappear.

During many periods in history, investing was much more challenging than what we saw in the last part of the 20th century. In my opinion, many changes, such as the United States having to compete in a global economy, terrorism, and the enormous debt the United States has undertaken, will make investing more difficult in the future.

Too much risk exists, and if you are retired you will not get another chance to earn it back if you lose it. So, if you do not have the proper training, seek qualified assistance.

If you are not going to manage your investments, who should? I believe you should use a financial services professional. If you did not read the first part of the book, go back to Part I and read Chapter 3, "Choosing a Financial Services Professional." As you will see, it is important to make sure you are working with someone who is well qualified to handle your situation—someone who will see the big picture and not give advice or make decisions for you without thinking through all of the possible ramifications.

This segment will help you understand what the investment world is made up of and how it works. I believe it is important that you have an understanding of the investment process. The more you know, the more likely you will be comfortable with what is happening with your investments.

Types of Investments and Terminology

The investment world consists of many different types of investments. The following terminology describes common types of investments and is heard quite often. It would be good if you are familiar with these terms.

Certificates of Deposit (CDs). Usually called a CD, a certificate of deposit is a short- to medium-term instrument (one month to five years) that is issued by a bank or savings and loan association. CDs pay more interest than most other bank accounts. However, once deposited your money must remain in the CD for the entire term, as there is usually a penalty for early withdrawal. A CD with a longer term usually pays a higher rate of interest because you are allowing the use of your money for a longer period. It is important to know that CDs are insured by the FDIC (Federal Deposit Insurance Corporation) up to $100,000 and offer a fixed rate of return. They do not protect against a rising cost of living. The FDIC insurance on CDs applies if the bank becomes insolvent, but does not protect market value. Other types of investments are not insured and their principal and yield may fluctuate with the market conditions.

Money Market Fund. A money market fund is a mutual fund that invests in short-term corporate and government debt and passes the interest payments on to shareholders. A key feature of money market funds is that their market value does not change, making them an ideal place to earn current market interest with a high degree of liquidity. An important fact to keep in mind is that an investment in a money market fund is not insured or guaranteed by the FDIC (Federal Deposit Insurance Corporation) or any other government agency. Although the fund seeks to preserve the value of your investment at $1 per share, it is possible to lose money by investing in a money market fund.

Corporate Bonds. Corporate bonds are fixed-income investments issued by corporations. When you invest in a corporate bond, you lend the corporation a set amount of money. For the use of your money, you are paid a stated rate of interest over the life of the bond, and your principal is returned when the bonds are "called," or mature. However, if you sell your bond prior to maturity, you may receive the same, more, or less than you paid for it. A bond's yield, price, and total return may change daily and are based on changes in interest rates, market conditions, and other economic and political news, and on the quality and maturity of the bond. In general, bond prices rise when interest rates fall and decline when interest rates rise. The effect is usually more pronounced for longer term bonds. If you sell your bond before maturity, you may incur a gain or a loss.

Municipal Bonds. A municipal bond is a debt obligation of a state or local government entity that supports general government needs or special projects. The earnings are tax-exempt for federal tax purposes, and if you buy one from the state you reside in the earnings are also state tax exempt.

Convertible Bonds. Convertible bonds offer the advantages of both stocks and bonds. A convertible bond is a fixed-income investment that can be converted at the holder's option into a specified number of shares of common stock of the issuing company at a pre-set price. Like ordinary bonds, convertible bonds carry a fixed interest rate that the issuing company is obligated to pay over the life of the bond. Convertibles generally pay interest semi-annually.

Common Stocks. Common stocks represent ownership in publicly traded companies and are sold in shares. Some companies grow very slowly and typically pay out most of their earnings in dividends; these are considered income stocks. Other companies grow very rapidly, reinvesting most of their earnings back into the company. These are considered growth stocks. It is important to understand that investments are subject to market risks including potential loss of the principal invested. Yields and prices will fluctuate along with the market and other economic conditions. Securities may be worth less than the original cost when sold.

Preferred Stocks. Preferred stocks, like common stocks, are considered equity investments because they represent ownership of a corporation. However, preferred stocks are quite different from common stocks since preferred stocks offer no growth potential. Preferred stocks pay a stated dividend rate that is usually declared and paid quarterly by the issuing corporation. In the event the issuing company incurs financial difficulties, preferred shareholders will be paid before common shareholders.

Mutual Funds. A mutual fund is an investment company that owns a variety of investments in a profession-ally managed and diversified portfolio. Depending on the objective of the fund, a mutual fund can own domestic and international stocks and bonds, utility stocks, tax-free bonds, and other marketable securities. When you invest in a mutual fund, your money is pooled together with money from thousands of other investors who have similar investment objectives. A money manager then invests the money from these investors into securities that will help the fund meet its stated objectives. When purchasing shares in a mutual fund, obtain a prospectus from your advisor for more complete information about investments, including investment objectives, risks, and charges and expenses. Please read the prospectus carefully before you invest.

Annuity. An annuity is composed of a series of regular payments, usually from an insurance company. The annuity is guaranteed by the insurance company (guarantees are subject to the ability of the issuer to pay claims) to continue for a specific time, usually the annuitant's lifetime, in exchange for a single payment or a series of payments to the company. Annuities grow tax deferred and are not taxed until payments are received. Most annuities carry a surrender charge that you will incur if you withdraw your money before the maturity date. There are many types of annuities. Here are three popular types of annuities.

1. A *deferred annuity* defers payments from the insurance company to sometime in the future. You give the insurance company your money now and they will pay you a stated rate of interest for an agreed amount of time. Upon the expiration of the period

you have four choices. You can receive all of your money back with the interest earned. The interest would be subject to tax in the year it is received. You can continue the annuity at the current crediting rate of interest being offered by the insurance company. You can begin taking payments over an agreed upon period. Or you can exchange your money tax deferred into another annuity.

2. When you purchase an *immediate annuity,* payments begin right away and continue over the period agreed upon between you and the insurance company.

3. With a *variable annuity,* payments do not begin until you request them, and the payments may change according to the relative investment success of the underlying investments. Variable annuities are allowed to invest in stock and bond sub accounts.

Brokerage Accounts. A brokerage account is a cash-management account into which investors deposit money in order to buy or sell securities. There must be enough money in the account to cover the trade at the time of its execution or the investor must be able to pay for the trade within three days (which is called the settlement date). Some brokerage firms accept credit cards to fund cash accounts, but most require cash or a personal check. Variations are known as margin and discretionary accounts.

Stock Market. The stock market is really just a big store where everyone goes to buy and sell their stock. The main players in the stock market are the exchanges. Exchanges are where the sellers are matched with buyers to both facilitate trading and to help set the price of the shares. The primary exchanges are the NASDAQ, the New York Stock Exchange (NYSE), all of the ECNs (electronic communication networks), and a few other regional exchanges like the American Stock Exchange and the Pacific Stock Exchange. Whenever someone sells a stock, someone else has to be buying the stock. Each transaction needs a buyer and a seller.

Adjusted Basis. Your basis is used to determine the taxable gain or loss when you sell an investment. The basis is usually what you pay for the investment, although special rules apply to assets you inherit or receive as a gift. Your basis can be adjusted while you own property. When stock or mutual fund shares are involved, your adjusted basis is the cost of the shares plus any brokerage commissions and any capital gain or dividend distributions that are reinvested into the stock or mutual fund. With real estate, your basis will be adjusted when you make improvements or invest more money into the property.

Dividends. Dividends are a portion of company earnings paid out to stockholders. Dividends are declared by a company's board of directors and paid quarterly. Most are paid as cash, but they are sometimes paid in the form of additional shares of stock.

Individual Retirement Account (IRA). A tax-sheltered account ideal for retirement investing because it permits investment earnings to accumulate untaxed until they are withdrawn. The contribution limit for 2004 is $3,000 per year unless you are age 50 or older—then you are allowed to contribute $3,500. In 2005, these numbers increase to $4,000 per year and $4,500 if you are 50 or older. If you withdraw money from your IRA before age 59½ penalties usually will apply. However, exceptions to the penalty are available if certain criteria are met. Speak to your tax advisor about these exceptions.

Capital Gain. The profit from the sale of property such as stocks, mutual fund shares, and real estate. The gains from the sale of assets owned for 12 months or less are "short-term gains" and are taxed at ordinary income tax rates. For most assets owned more than 12 months before selling, profits are considered "long-term gains" and are taxed at a top rate of 15%, unless you are in the 10% or 15% tax bracket, in which case a flat 5% rate applies. In 2008, the 5% rate falls to 0%. These rates are subject to change by Congress at anytime.

Capital Loss. The loss from the sale of assets such as stocks, bonds, mutual funds, and real estate. Such losses are used to offset capital gains, and up to $3,000 of excess losses can be deducted against other income, such as your salary or retirement distributions.

Asset Allocation. Asset allocation is the process of dividing investments among different kinds of asset classes, such as stocks, bonds, international equities, international bonds, commodities (gold, oil, gas, timber, etc.), real estate, cash, etc. The goal is to diversify portfolio investment holdings across different asset classes that have low correlation to one another. In other words, if one asset class is down, historically a different asset class may be up. Asset allocation makes good sense but it does not ensure a profit or protect against losses in declining markets.

Diversification. An investment strategy meant to minimize risk by diversifying among many holdings. Diversification and risk are directly related to each other because the more you diversify your portfolio, the less risk you have. To illustrate, say all of your money is invested in the stock of one particular company—XYZ Corp. This would be a risky proposition for three main reasons. First, the value of XYZ's stock could be adversely affected by weakness in the overall stock market. Second, the value of the stock could suffer if its industry as a whole falls onto hard times. And third, even if both the stock market and the industry are doing great, the value of XYZ Corp.'s stock could tumble for a variety of other reasons unique to the company, such as an unexpected shutdown of its plants, the loss of a key customer, or even the death of one of its key executives. However, if you invest in eight different companies, the odds of a large drop in your portfolio's overall value are reduced.

The Investment Process

These terms are not all inclusive, but are good terms to know and understand. When you are working with your financial advisor, you will probably hear some of these terms. Now let's concentrate on how the investment process works.

After you find an advisor you are comfortable with, the process begins. Before you can begin to know how to invest your money, some important factors need to be identified.

First, what are your goals? In other words, what do you plan to use the money for? Are you saving for a second home? Is your main goal to use your money to fund your retirement? Some people have a goal to fund their grandchildren's education. Many possibilities exist. The first thing you need to do is clarify your goals.

Second, when do you need to withdraw the money? Do you require a certain amount each month? Maybe you do not have a need for ten years, so right now you want your money to grow. Some people may never need their investment money because they collect large pensions. The time frame is very important to know when determining investment strategies.

Third, how much risk can you tolerate? If you see the value of your investment account go down 20%, would it make you miserable? Sometimes percents are deceiving—let me restate the 20% another way. How would you feel if you had $500,000 invested and it dropped in value to $400,000?

Many people understand true dollars better than a percent. My experience tells me that if you have not invested during a downturn in the market, such as the one we experienced in 2000–2, you really do not have a proper feel for how much risk you can tolerate. People who thought they could handle it struggled painfully with their losses. This was not their fault. How could they know without experiencing it? Nonetheless, you still have to try to understand how you would feel about such a change.

A financial services professional should have a risk assessment you can complete to help determine your tolerance for risk. Because this assessment cannot replace true-life experience, I always try to err on the conservative side.

After determining your goals, time frame, and risk tolerance, the next step is to select your asset allocation and make sure it is diversified. As mentioned above, asset allocation is the process of dividing investments among different kinds of asset classes such as stocks, bonds, international equities, international bonds, real estate, commodities, cash, etc. Among these asset classes, you need to diversify your investments. In other words, don't buy just one stock or bond. To be diversified within an asset class such as stocks, my rule of thumb is to own at least eight stocks. An easy way to be diversified is to buy a mutual fund. It is common for one mutual fund to own many stocks.

For each asset class you invest in, make sure you have enough holdings to be diversified. Even though a mutual fund may own many stocks, they may all be the same type of stock, such as small companies. Proper diversification requires you to have large stocks and small stocks as well as dividend-paying stocks and nondividend-paying stocks. Each asset class has more than one style in it, so it is important to know what the styles are and what you are purchasing to avoid buying all of the same type of investment.

I believe it is essential that you allocate your investments into many different asset classes. The traditional view of many advisors I have observed is to invest in U.S. stocks, U.S. bonds, and international stocks. While this is partial asset allocation, it ignores many of the other asset classes mentioned above. The more asset classes you can use, the less volatile your portfolio should be. How you allocate your funds to these asset classes is dictated by your risk tolerance. Generally, the more conservative you are the less you will invest in the riskier asset classes, such as stocks and commodities, and the more you will invest in bonds and cash.

Investing Tax Efficiently

Over the last few years, more attention has been paid to investing tax efficiently. Tax efficient investing can be done in more ways than one. First, you can buy certain investments that are more tax efficient than others. For example, many mutual funds are now available that are managed to minimize the tax impact to the investor. Second, if you are in a high tax bracket, you may buy a municipal bond. A municipal bond can avoid federal tax and, if it is issued by your home state, it can avoid state taxes. Third, tax efficiency can be achieved by owning your investments in the correct accounts. For example, you may want to own a taxable corporate bond in your IRA because the tax will be deferred until you withdraw money from your IRA. You may also want to own a common stock outside of a retirement plan so that when you sell it, and incur a capital gain, you pay the tax on it at the current low rate of 15%. If you had the stock inside of your retirement plan, there would be no tax when you sold it, but it would be subject to a higher ordinary income tax rate when you withdraw money from the retirement plan.

And yet another possibility exists if after your spouse passed away a family or credit trust was created and funded with their assets. (See the "AB Trust Wills" section in Chapter 4, "Estate Planning for Married Couples.") This trust is generally funded to the amount the law allows to pass free of estate tax. For 2004, this amount is $1,500,000. If you have this situation, the assets that are in the credit or family trust would be invested for growth, while the assets you have in your own name would be invested more conservatively. The assets in the trust will not be subject to estate tax at your death, so if your estate were to grow it would be better to have the growth in the trust. The goal of this strategy is to reduce the overall estate tax paid. Once again, before acting on any of these strategies, make sure you consult with your advisor.

Annuities

Annuities have been around for a long time, and many people are not sure if an annuity is appropriate for them. This topic is debated heavily by financial service professionals themselves. The truth of the matter is everybody's situation is different and each needs to be analyzed individually.

While variable annuities can provide nice features, such as tax deferral and investments in the equity markets, they also may have high expense ratios. Fixed annuities are a savings vehicle that offers competitive returns, but are they appropriate for people with very low incomes who are in low tax brackets? These are a few of the questions that you and your advisor need to address when determining if annuities are right for you.

Chapter Twenty-seven

Income Taxes

You are not expected to be an expert on income taxes, but, once again, there are a few valuable items you should know. First, if your tax situation is complicated in any manner you should use a professional tax preparer. Even if your situation is not complicated, do not prepare your own return if you are not sure of what you are doing. I have seen too many situations where people do it themselves and miss one or two items that will cost them more in tax than the cost of having a preparer do the return. Second, be organized. When you start to receive tax documents in January set up a separate file folder and label it "Current Tax Information." File all of your current information in this folder so that when you visit your tax preparer you will have your information ready to go.

The following four tax planning ideas may or may not apply to you. They are included because if they do apply, they could be very valuable to you.

Taxation of Social Security Benefits

Depending on your total annual income, a portion of your Social Security benefit may be subject to income tax. If the total of your taxable pensions, wages, interest (taxable and tax-exempt), dividends, and other taxable income plus half of your Social Security benefit is more than the base amount, some of your benefits will be taxable. The base is $25,000 for a single person and $32,000 for those who are married filing jointly.

> **Example:** *The simple chart in Figure 6 shows an individual's tax situation for the year. Our goal is to calculate what portion of the Social Security benefit will be subject to tax. This individual has three sources of income: dividends, municipal bond interest, and Social Security benefits. The total income this individual received was $30,000, but this is not the number used for tax purposes. To compute the amount of Social Security benefit subject to tax we must add together the dividends, the municipal bond interest, and one-half of the Social Security benefits. As you can see from the chart this equals $25,000. Because it is not higher than the base amount allowed for a single person, none of the Social Security benefit is taxable. What happens when we add another $1,000 of interest income? This would cause $500 of the Social Security benefit to be taxable. The law states that for every $1 of income over $25,000, 50% of a Social Security dollar will become taxable. And if the income is over $34,000, 85% of each dollar*

over $34,000 would be subject to tax until every dollar
of Social Security income has been taxed.

Figure 6. Taxation of Social Security Benefits

	Total income	Calculation of Social Security benefit subject to tax
Dividend income	$15,000	$15,000
Municipal bond interest	$5,000	$5,000
Social security income	$10,000	$5,000
Subtotals	$30,000	$25,000
Additional interest income		$1,000
Modified income for Social Security benefit subject to tax		$26,000
Social security benefit taxable (50% of the amount over $25,000) (85% of the amount over $34,000)	N/A	$500

If the modified income amount above was $35,000, then the taxable amount of Social Security benefit would be $850 ($1000 x 85%).

This may not seem immediately significant to you, but not paying attention can significantly increase your taxes. In some situations, say if you live in a state that carries a higher tax rate (like Minnesota), your marginal tax rate could be as high as 60%. That is right—60%! When you see a tax percent that high, you must consider tax planning.

Do you need to know how to compute this? No. I just think you should be aware of it. Ask your tax preparer if your Social Security benefits are being taxed. If the preparer says yes, ask what you can do about it. If you are using a quality tax preparer, they will know how to advise you. The main idea is to plan to reduce the amount of income you report on your tax return. Restructuring your investments so they are more tax efficient can accomplish this. Another possibility is to reduce the amount you withdraw from retirement plans and draw money from a nontaxable source such as a money market account.

Tax Bracket Planning

The United States has a progressive tax rate system. This means that the more income you have, the higher the tax rates you are subjected to. The current (2004) rates are 10%, 15%, 25%, 28%, 33% and 35%.

In most cases, people do not like to pay taxes at any rate. However, depending on your situation it may not be so bad to pay tax at a 10% or a 15% rate. Most often, this is relevant for people who have children and who have money in retirement accounts like individual retirement accounts (IRAs) and annuities. Taxes do not have to be paid on these accounts until funds are withdrawn. Many times I see a person is paying very little income tax because their taxable income is low even though they have substantial assets. They are not using their entire 10% and 15% brackets. I will suggest that they consider withdrawing additional amounts from their IRA or annuities to create income and pay more taxes. Why? you may ask. Because if they have children it is likely the children are working and are in a higher tax bracket, say 25%. If the parent were to die without withdrawing all of the funds from their IRA, it will usually go to their children, who will pay income tax on the funds at possibly a much higher tax rate. Another reason to use up your low tax brackets is that you never know how long the government will keep tax rates this low.

Charitable Giving

If you are a charitable person and make gifts to churches or other nonprofit organizations, a more tax efficient way may be found for you to make your gifts. If you happen to own investments such as stock that is highly appreciated, you may want to donate the stock to your favorite charity. The tax law allows you to donate property such as a stock to a charitable organization and take a deduction for the full fair market value of the stock. The good news is you do not have to pay tax on the gain attributable to the stock. As an example, if you have a stock that is worth $3,000 and you paid $1,000 for it, your taxable gain would be $2,000 when you sold it. If you donate the stock to a charity, you do not have to pay tax on the gain. Most charities have brokerage accounts, so making this type of donation has become quite common. If you have appreciated investments and make regular contributions to charity, this idea is for you.

Medical Expenses

Are you paying a large amount of medical expenses or nursing home costs for a family member? If you are you may have large medical deductions on your tax return. If the deductions are large enough, they may reduce your taxable income to zero, or even make it negative.

This planning idea goes back to using your low tax brackets. If you find yourself in this situation, consider withdrawing enough money from IRAs or annuities to use up these low tax brackets. At a minimum, withdraw enough to bring your taxable income back to zero. Ideally, use your 10% and 15% brackets. This situation may not happen often, but if it does take advantage of it.

Important: To take advantage of any of these tax planning suggestions you must meet with your tax preparer at least 1–2 months before the year ends. These suggestions require implementation before December 31 each year.

Chapter Twenty-eight

Insurance Issues

Many different types of insurance are available for all sorts of purposes. In Part I, Chapter 5, we discussed life, disability, and long-term care insurance in depth. In this section, property insurance for your home and car, umbrella personal liability, and health insurance are covered, including Medicare and Medigap insurance. In addition, we will revisit life and long-term care insurance to review how they might apply to you now as a single person.

Insurance is an essential part of finances. I advocate having it when you need it, but not overpaying for it.

Homeowners' Insurance

For many people their home is one of their most valuable assets. This is likely true for you, and protecting this asset is very important to your long-term financial health. If you are not familiar with this type of insurance, I hope that after reading this you will have a much better understanding of homeowners insurance. The following questions will be answered:

- What types and levels of coverage are available?

- What does a policy cover and not cover?

- What do you look for in a policy and how to you control the cost?

Types and Levels of Coverage. The homeowners' policy provides protection against the financial consequences of personal losses. It provides two types of coverage: property and liability. The paragraphs below detail several types of property and liability coverage.

- *Property coverage* pays for the dwelling. This insurance amount applies to your house and attached structures. The maximum amount insured is based on the value of the home and the cost to replace it.

- *Other structures coverage* applies to detached structures, such as a garage or storage shed. The limit of coverage for other structures is set at 10% of the dwelling; however you can purchase a higher limit.

- *Personal property coverage* provides coverage for the personal property of the insured. Special limits apply to certain types of property, and certain property is excluded from coverage. The overall limit for coverage is 50% of the dwelling limit. This coverage can be modified in several ways with endorsements. Make sure you choose replacement cost protection instead of actual cash value for your personal property. This will allow you to replace the damaged property at its current cost.

- *Loss-of-use coverage* applies in the event you were to temporarily lose the use of your home. Payment would be made for expenses incurred to live elsewhere following a loss that makes the home unsuitable for living. Another method used to determine payment for loss of use is fair rental value, which is the amount of rent that could reasonably be charged for the premises less any expenses that do not continue while the premises are unsuitable for living.

- *Liability coverage* offers protection from covered claims made against you or a resident family member for property damage or bodily injury. This coverage is broken into two parts:

  1. *Personal liability coverage* pays when you or a resident family member is found legally responsible for damage to the property of others or injuries to persons who are not members of your household; however, payments cannot exceed your coverage limits. For example, a mailman slips on the ice on your doorstep and is injured. If you are found legally responsible your personal liability coverage will pay for the damages (e.g., medical expenses, lost wages) incurred by the mailman. Personal liability has a basic limit of $100,000 per occurrence, which may increase for an additional premium. I suggest having $300,000 to $500,000 of coverage.

2. *Medical payments coverage* will pay the necessary medical expenses for bodily injury of others. Coverage applies to accidents that occur on the insured's premises or any location when caused by action of the insured. The coverage has a basic limit of $1,000 per person. The insured may select higher limits.

Your insurance policy likely offers one of three options for levels of coverage:

- *Replacement cost* pays the policyholder the cost of the damaged property without deduction for depreciation but limited to a maximum dollar amount.

- *Guaranteed replacement cost* pays the full cost of replacing damaged property without a deduction for depreciation and without a dollar limit. This coverage is not available in all states and some companies limit the coverage to 120% of the cost of rebuilding the property. This option gives you protection against such things as a sudden increase in construction costs due to a shortage of building materials.

- *Actual cash* pays the policyholder an amount equal to the replacement value of damaged property minus an allowance for depreciation. Unless a homeowner's policy specifies that property be covered for its replacement value, the coverage is for actual cash value.

I believe homeowners should buy the guaranteed replacement cost coverage. It will cost more, but is well worthwhile if you ever have to use it.

What is covered and what is not covered? Your home-owner's policy will generally cover the loss of your belongings in the event of theft, fire, and other casualties. Your insurance policy will generally pay for all or part of the cost to repair or replace property that is destroyed or damaged. You are also protected against liability lawsuits as mentioned previously. Homeowner's coverage will normally cover damage from:

- Smoke
- Fire
- Vandalism
- Theft
- Windstorm
- Hail
- Riot
- Falling objects
- Explosion
- Ice and snow
- Plumbing freeze-ups
- Furnace breakdown
- Hot water heater breakdown
- Power surges

This list is not all-inclusive, but it should give you an idea of what is covered.

More important is to know what may not be covered. You may assume your policy will cover everything, but you may be surprised at some of the items that are not covered. Have you ever spoken with someone who has experienced a sewer backup in their home? Let me tell you, the story would not be pretty. Unless you have a special rider for sewer backup and sump pump failure, you will not be covered. Depending what you have on the lower level of your home, you could be looking at replacing carpeting and furniture. Most people do not realize this until it is too late.

Do you own any expensive items such as jewelry, guns, antiques, artwork, or fine furs? Most insurance policies will cover these items but only to a total maximum of $1,000 to $2,000. If your valuables are worth more than this, you should attach a rider to your policy that will cover the additional value. An estimated cost would be $15 for every additional $1,000 of value you would like to insure.

Is your dog named Fluffy or Spike? Most dogs do not cause a problem for insurance, but some may. Certain breeds of dogs have reputations for being aggressive and likely will *not* be covered by your policy. The insurance industry is not happy with all of the dog bites they have had to pay for in recent years. Also, if you have a dog with a calmer reputation (such as a poodle or cocker spaniel) and the dog has ever bitten anyone, you may not get coverage.

The bottom line is that if you have an aggressive dog, it may cost you more than it is worth to keep it. Consider getting rid of the dog before it costs you or someone else an arm and leg.

Are you handy around the house? If not, hire a fix-it man, because if you neglect to properly maintain your home, you may not be covered. If you have water leaks, rodents, termites, etc., it is your responsibility to take care of these issues before they become a real problem. If you are not sure if you have a problem, have a home inspector come and check your house every few years.

This list of concerns is not all-inclusive, but these items are the most common. If any of them apply to you, please take appropriate action.

Taking Inventory. One last item you should consider is how to document your property to substantiate what you own. If you have a fire and all of your property is destroyed, do you really think you could recall all the items that you had? I know that I could not, but who could? This is the reason it is important to document what you have. While this can be a chore and I would guess most people do not do it, taking an inventory is very important. There are two ways to do it. First, you can make out a handwritten list that details all of your personal belongings. Ask your property insurance salesperson if they can give you some type of preprinted inventory form that will make this task easier for you. Begin with one room and after everything is recorded move on to the next until you have documented every room in the house. To supplement your handwritten list, I would suggest that you take photographs of your property, especially the more expensive items. If you have really expensive items, obtain an appraisal. Your inventory, appraisals, photographs, etc., should be stored away from your home preferably in a safety deposit box. The second way is to use a video camera. Over the last 20 years, video cameras have become popular, and it seems that most households now have one. The nice part about the video camera versus a regular camera is the audio, which allows you to do a commentary as you are filming your household goods. Make sure to date your video with the dating feature on the camera. Begin by taking a wide-angle shot of the whole room, and then focus in on each of the items. As you film each item, you can give a brief explanation of what it is, when you purchased it and how much it cost. Make sure that each area you are filming is well lit so there is no doubt about what you are documenting. This is the best way to inventory because it is easy and leaves a great record of what you own.

Shopping for a Policy. When you are shopping for homeowners' insurance you need to do some research to make sure you are getting a good rate. Many insurance companies offer discounts, and they are not all the same. You need to ask your property insurance agent what discounts are available. The following are some helpful hints to consider when seeking and purchasing homeowners' insurance:

- *Select a higher deductible.* The deductible amount is the amount that you agree to self-insure. In other words, if you have a $500 deductible, you are responsible for paying the first $500 toward the repair of any damages. Deductibles generally start at $250 and can go much higher from there. A higher deductible will result in a lower premium. For example, your premium may go down 12% if you change from a $250 to a $500 deductible. If you raise your deductible to $1,000, the premium could be reduced by as much as 24%. Whatever deductible you choose, make sure you can pay it if need be. I generally recommend a $1,000 deductible for two reasons: it helps keep premiums down and it has been my experience that if you turn in a lot of low-dollar-amount claims, the insurance company will either cancel you or raise your premiums.

- *Buy your homeowners and auto insurance from the same company.* Many companies offer a multiline discount if you purchase two or more policies from them.

- *Stop smoking.* Some companies offer lower premiums if the residents of the house do not smoke.

- *Check discounts for seniors.* If you are age 55 or over you may qualify for a discount of as much as 10%.

- *Insure the house and not the land.* The land that your house sits on is not going to be damaged by theft, fire, or windstorm. Do not include it in the value of the property to be insured.

- *Stay with the same insurer.* If you stay with the same company for many years, some insurers will grant you a discount of 5% to 10%.

- *Improve your home security.* This may reduce your insurance cost as well as allow you to sleep better at night. Install deadbolts, a security system, and smoke detectors. Depending on what you install, some companies will give you discounts as high as 15% to 20%.

- *Shop around.* Ask family and friends whom they use or check in the yellow pages. Another option is to look at local advertising.

I hope that these tips help you save money on your homeowners' insurance policy. Remember to review your policy annually and update it if you make any major purchases or improvements to your home.

Auto Insurance

Your car may not be as valuable as your house, but it is just as important to have the proper insurance coverage. The insurance protection on a car is actually more important from a liability perspective. The potential dollar loss is high if you were to be sued for causing an automobile accident and not being properly insured. To help you gain a better understanding of car insurance this section will cover the following:

- What types and levels of coverage are available?
- How do you control the cost of a policy?

Types and Levels of Coverage. There are six basic types of auto insurance coverage. The following definitions from the Better Business Bureau describe each type of coverage:

- *Bodily injury liability.* pays your legal defense costs and claims against you if your car injures or kills someone. Covers family members living with you and others driving with your permission.

- *Property damage liability.* Pays your legal defense costs and claims against you if your car damages another's property, but does not cover your property, including your auto.

- *Medical payments or personal injury protection.* Pays medical expenses resulting from an accident, for you and others riding in your car. Also pays for you or your family members injured while riding in another's car or while walking.

- *Collision.* Pays for repairs of damage to your car caused by a collision with another vehicle or any other object, regardless of who was responsible.

- *Comprehensive physical damage.* Pays for damages to your car resulting from theft, fire, hail, vandalism, or a variety of other causes.

- *Uninsured or underinsured motorist.* Pays for costs related to injuries or property damage to you or your family members and guests in your car caused by an uninsured, underinsured, or hit-and-run driver.

What types of coverage should you have? In all but four states—Florida, New Hampshire, Tennessee, and Wisconsin —you are required to have bodily injury liability and property damage liability coverage. Some states require you to have medical payments or personal injury protection and uninsured or underinsured motorist, but not all. Collision and comprehensive are optional coverage.

How much coverage should you have for bodily injury liability and property damage liability insurance? Most states require a minimum amount. These amounts are too low and you will normally see them listed like this: 25/50/10. The first two numbers, 25/50, represent bodily injury coverage. The 25 represents $25,000 coverage per person and the 50 represents $50,000 coverage per accident. The last amount, 10, represents $10,000 of property damage liability.

Most insurance professionals recommend purchasing coverage of 100/300/50. You may want to consider coverage in excess of this along with an umbrella insurance policy (which is discussed in the next section).

Should you purchase the types of insurance that are

not required? First, medical payments or personal injury protection should be purchased unless you have extensive health insurance coverage for yourself and family. Even then, your health insurance will not cover passengers who are not related to you if they are hurt in an accident in your car. Nevertheless, if you have good health insurance and usually drive with just family members, you may be able to go without this type of coverage.

Second, uninsured or underinsured motorist may not be needed if you live in a no-fault state where your insurance will be required to cover your losses even if the other driver was at fault. If you do not live in a no-fault state, I believe you should purchase this coverage. Look for coverage of around $250,000 per person and $500,000 per accident to cover potential bodily injury protection.

Third, I suggest you purchase collision and comprehensive insurance unless your car is worth only $2,000 or less. I use this figure as a rule of thumb, but you still need to make your own decision and discuss it with your property insurance agent.

Shopping for a policy. Now that you understand the coverage, how can you control the premiums on your policy? There are many possibilities if you follow the suggestions that follow:

- *Higher deductibles.* Just as with homeowner's insurance, the higher the deductible on auto insurance, the lower the premium. In my opinion $500 is the lowest I would go, and if you can afford it, consider a $1,000 deductible.

* *Comprehensive and collision.* Do not purchase if your car is worth less than $2,000.

* *Low mileage discounts.* Check to see if your company gives discounts if you drive less than a predetermined number of miles each year.

* *Good driving record.* Avoid accidents and traffic tickets for a period of three years and receive a discount. It also pays to understand what road signs mean, unlike the ladies in this story...

A highway patrol officer was sitting on the side of the road when he saw a car come by at 22 miles per hour. He starts thinking to himself that a driver going too slow is just as dangerous as a speeding driver. He decides to pull the car over. After the car is stopped, he approaches the driver's side door and notices there are five older ladies in the car. The passengers are all white in the face and look scared to death. The driver of the car tells the officer that she was not speeding and was going exactly the speed limit. "What seems to be the problem?" she asked. "Ma'am," the officer replies, "You were not speeding, you were driving much slower than the speed limit and that can be dangerous to other drivers." The driver responds, "Slower than the speed limit, that could not be, I was going 22 just like the sign said." The officer catches on and, trying to control his laugh, explains to her, "22 is the route number, not the speed limit." The woman was embarrassed and thanked the officer for pointing out the problem. The officer said "You're welcome, but before I let you go, I have to ask if everyone in the car is okay. Your passengers look a bit shaken. They have not said a word." The woman responds, "They should be all right in a minute, officer. We just got off route 115."

- *Nonsmoker discount.* It does not pay to smoke.

- *Drivers education courses.* Go back to school and get a discount.

- *Be proud of your age.* Drivers over age 50 receive a discount.

- *Location considerations.* If you live in a rural area your premium costs should be lower.

- *Multiple policy discounts.* Buy at least two types of insurance from the same company and receive a discount.

- *Loyalty discounts.* Stay with your insurance company for many years and they will reward you for your loyalty.

- *Buy a less expensive car.* The less valuable your car, the cheaper it will be to insure.

- *Comparison shop.* Talk to an independent agent who can shop many insurance companies to help you find the best price.

This list is not all-inclusive, but it is a good start. The insurance agent you are working with should also be able to suggest discounts for which you may qualify. Do not be afraid to ask, and make sure you are getting everything to which you are entitled.

Umbrella Insurance

In the lawsuit-happy society we live in, do you ever think about being sued? Well, if you do not, you should. Lawsuits can result from no fault of your own, such as a person slipping on the sidewalk and hurting themselves. On the other hand, they may come from an auto accident that was your fault. The main point is that you are not immune from becoming a party to a lawsuit. Have you ever thought about the financial problems a lawsuit could cause you? If you have any assets you could lose in a lawsuit, you should have extra protection. How do you get extra protection? You purchase an umbrella personal liability policy.

Why does this insurance have such a peculiar name? The name exists because this insurance acts like an umbrella over your auto and homeowners' liability policies, providing extra protection. Your auto and homeowners' policy may provide you with $300,000 and $100,000 of liability protection, depending on the liability amount you have purchased. If you purchase an umbrella policy, most insurance companies require you buy your umbrella, homeowners', and auto policies through them. They also require you to carry $300,000 to $500,000 of liability coverage on your house and auto. This would then be the deductible for the umbrella personal liability policy. The coverage provided by the umbrella policy begins when the limit of your auto or homeowner policy is reached.

> *Example: Let's say that you have $300,000 of bodily injury liability protection with your auto insurance policy. You cause a car accident and someone is seriously injured. They sue you for $700,000 and win. Your auto policy will pay $300,000, but where will you get the other $400,000? This amount would be covered by your umbrella personal liability policy.*

What does an umbrella policy cover? Up to the limits of the policy it will cover the following:

- Claims of personal injuries or property damage caused by you, family members, or unsafe conditions on your property, for which you are found liable.

- Personal liability coverage for events that happen on or off your property.

- Additional protection over and above the liability limits of your homeowners' and auto policies.

- Protection against nonbusiness related personal injury claims, such as slander, libel, and false arrest.

- Legal defense costs for a covered loss.

Umbrella personal liability policies do not cover everything, however. The following are some items that are generally excluded:

- Intentional damage caused by you or a member of your household.

- Claims from business or professional pursuits.

- Liability for claims you accepted under a contract or agreement.

- Liability related to the use of nontraditional transportation, such as airplanes or jet skis and the maintenance thereof.

- Damage to your own property.

- Liabilities resulting from war.

- Damage covered under a workers compensation policy.

How much of an umbrella should you buy, and how much does it cost? Many people will purchase policies that give them coverage in the $1,000,000 to $2,000,000 range. You must judge for yourself, but this is normally what I suggest, and the cost of the policy is relatively cheap. You can very likely buy $1,000,000 of coverage for less than $200. Check with your property insurance agent and see if this makes sense for you.

Life Insurance

You may have some existing life insurance in place. Your spouse and you may have had a survivorship (second to die) policy in place when your spouse passed away. If so, it was probably intended to pay estate taxes upon the second death. This policy should be kept so that it can perform its original purpose, paying estate taxes. If you have a policy on just yourself, you need to analyze why you have it and whether it makes sense to keep it. If you do not have a policy, you should determine if you have a need for one.

Why would you need to have a life insurance policy? I can think of three good reasons. First, you may have children who depend on you and need your support. Generally, this is a need that you would cover until you believe the children will no longer have to rely on you. For most people, this happens when the children leave school and enter the workforce. Second, you may have other family members, such as parents or a less fortunate sibling, who need your support. This need would very likely continue until they die. Third, your estate may be subject to the estate tax. To see if this is a problem, review Chapter 4, "Estate Planning for Married Couples," in Part I. In addition, there is an in-depth discussion of life insurance in Chapter 5, Part I, which may help you understand the types of insurance that are available.

Three possible needs for insurance have been identified. Now let's address how to insure each need. If your need is to take care of children until they are out of school, it would make sense to purchase term insurance because there is a definite end date to the need for the insurance. If the need is to take care of a family member or pay estate taxes, you should use one of the types of insurance that maintain a cash value. It is my belief that since the goal is not to build up a large cash value, but make sure a death benefit is available when you pass away, it would be wise to fund these two causes with universal life insurance. This would most likely provide you with the lowest premiums for the types of insurance that maintain a cash value.

Health Insurance

If you are age 65 or older and eligible for Medicare and Medigap insurance, obtaining health insurance will not be an issue for you. Also, if you are employed and have coverage with your employer, this will not apply. But if you need health insurance, there are some things you should know.

Private Health Insurance

Private health insurance is expensive and important. You need to make sure you get appropriate coverage and also pay attention to the cost. When shopping for a policy, the following components should be understood and considered:

- *Deductibles.* A $250 deductible is fairly common. The higher the deductible you agree to, the lower your premium. If you can afford it, consider a $500 or $1,000 deductible.

- *Copayments.* Cap out-of-pocket exposure to a level you can afford. $1,000 to $2,000 is common. Again, the higher the out-of-pocket maximum, the lower the premium.

- Cover at least 80% of both your medical and hospital bills once you meet your deductible.

- Do not exclude or limit coverage of preexisting conditions.

- Make sure your lifetime coverage is at least $1,000,000.

- Purchase a policy that is guaranteed renewable.

Some books suggest that you shop for health insurance on the Internet, but I believe you will be better off working with a professional in your area. Then, if problems arise you will have a person you can speak to face-to-face. Ask your accountant, attorney, or financial advisor for a referral. Any one of these individuals should be able to find you a qualified professional.

Long-Term Care Insurance

This topic was also covered thoroughly in Chapter 5 in

Part I. You are most likely alone now and if something were to happen to you there may be no one to stay home and help you out. You may be financially well off and be able to afford to hire help. If you can, that would be great. However, if you cannot afford it, purchasing long-term care coverage could allow you to stay in your home longer than you may have otherwise. Remember, the earlier in life you can apply, the better chance you have of being accepted and paying a lower premium.

Medicare

Health issues are becoming some of the most important issues of our time. Health care costs are increasing annually at above-inflation rates. The population of the United States is getting older by the day, and the need for health care will be ever increasing. The Medicare program is the major health insurance coverage for individuals age 65 and older in our country.

What is Medicare? It is a federal health insurance program designed for individuals age 65 and older, certain disabled individuals under age 65, and individuals with permanent kidney failure. It provides basic protection against the cost of health care. Many people believe that Medicare will cover all of their medical costs and long-term care, but this is simply not true. What is not covered by Medicare?

- Most nursing home care

- Dental care and dentures
- Routine checkups and the tests directly related to these checkups
- Most immunization shots
- Most prescription drugs
- Routine foot care
- Eyeglasses, hearing aids, or related testing
- Services outside the United States
- Luxuries in your hospital room, such as television and telephone

Because of these limitations many people own medical supplement policies known as Medigap policies. This topic will be covered after this section.

Medicare has two parts, known as A and B. Part A pays benefits for hospital and skilled nursing home care, and Part B helps pay for doctor bills and outpatient services. People enrolled in Medicare must pay a deductible fee. For hospitalization, Medicare Part A has a deductible for each hospital stay during the year. Services and deductibles for Part A and B are listed below. The amount of these deductibles usually increases each year.

Service benefits paid by Medicare Part A:

- Semiprivate hospital room and board
- Skilled nursing and rehabilitative services
- Blood transfusions during hospital stay

- Pain relief and symptom management during hospital stay
- Physical, occupational, and speech therapy
- Medical social services
- Skilled nursing facility care
- Part-time in-home skilled nursing care
- Hospice services

Medicare Part B is optional and requires a monthly premium. It covers certain medical and outpatient services, including physician care. The premium varies, and an annual deductible applies. After paying the deductible, Medicare B will pay 80% of Medicare-approved charges, and you are responsible for the remaining 20%.

Medicare Part B will pay for:

- Outpatient hospital procedures
- X-rays and lab tests
- Diagnostic tests
- Nursing and physician services
- Drugs for pain relief
- Home health aid
- Counseling services
- Prosthetic devices such as artificial limbs
- Flu and pneumonia shots

- Blood transfusions and medical equipment and kidney dialysis

- Limited ambulance transportation

Some specific requirements must be met before enrolling in Medicare Part B. It is a good idea to contact the Social Security Administration prior to turning age 65 for information about enrollment and about limitations on Medicare payments for specific services.

The deductibles on Medicare can be quite high, especially for hospital stays, as shown in the following tables. To help pay these deductibles, you should have a Medigap policy if you can afford one. Medigap is discussed in a later section.

Figure 7. Medicare Part A—Hospital Insurance (Amounts apply to each benefit period)

Hospital:	
Inpatient deductible	$876.00
Coinsurance days 61 through 90	$219.00 per day
Coinsurance days 91 through 150	$438.00 per day

Figure 8. Medicare Part B—Medical Insurance

Part B premium	$66.60 per month
Annual deductible	$100.00
Coinsurance	20% of approved charges

How do you sign up for Medicare? If you are already receiving Social Security benefit payments, you will automatically get a Medicare card in the mail about three months before your 65th birthday, along with an enrollment information package. The card will usually show that you are entitled to both Part A (Hospital Insurance) and Part B (Supplementary Medical Services) and indicate the beginning dates of your entitlement to each. If you do not want Part B, follow the instructions that come in the package.

The question you may have is whether you should enroll in Part B. In most cases, you should. If you are still employed by a company with 20 or more employees and you are covered under your employer's health insurance plan, you can wait. Your employer's insurance will continue to be your primary coverage, and you can elect Part B when you retire. When retirement does occur, apply for Part B to be effective the same date as your retirement, and there will be no penalties and no delays in obtaining Part B Medicare. It will be effective the date of your retirement.

If you have already retired, or work for a company with fewer than 20 employees, you should enroll in Part B. If you do not enroll, even though you have group health insurance, your coverage will be inadequate. Your group insurance is secondary to Medicare and will not pay the portion of the bill they estimate Part B Medicare would pay. In addition, if you refuse Part B Medicare when you become eligible at age 65, there will be penalties to pay when you realize you should not have refused it.

A premium payment is collected for Medicare Part B. It is usually paid by the individual either through deductions from their Social Security checks or by direct billing. However, if your income and resources are low enough, the state you reside in may pay your Medicare Part B premiums. Most people pay the same premium amount, although some beneficiaries may also pay premium surcharges because of delayed Medicare enrollment.

If you are not receiving Social Security benefits when you turn 65, you have to apply for Medicare coverage with the Social Security Administration. Call 1-800-772-1213 or visit your local Social Security office. If applying for Medicare, you should do so during your initial seven-month enrollment period. That period starts three months before the month you turn 65 and ends three months after. For Medicare to begin at age 65, enrollment must occur prior to the month you turn 65. For each month after, enrollment is delayed. Also, as mentioned earlier, if Part B is not elected by age 65, you will pay penalties.

New Medicare Prescription Drug Law

In December 2003, President George W. Bush signed into law a new Medicare Part D Prescription Drug benefit law. Under the new law, individuals can sign up for the Medicare Prescription Drug Plan beginning January 1, 2006.

Even though the new drug benefit will not start until 2006, a Medicare drug discount card will be available in June 2004. The new card is expected to offer an *average* 15% discount off the cost of prescription drugs. If your household income is below $12,569 for an individual or $16,862 for a married couple, you will get an additional $600 benefit from the card, which will help even more. Beneficiaries in each state will have a choice between two Medicare prescription drug discount cards. The prescription drug discount card must be purchased, but it will not cost more than $30 annually, and low-income beneficiaries will have their drug discount cards paid for by Medicare.

Beginning in January 2006, if you elect to enroll in the Medicare Part D Prescription Drug Plan you will pay a $35 monthly premium. The plan will also have an annual deductible of $250 before Medicare begins to pay. After the $250 deductible, you will be responsible for 25% of the next $2,000 spent on prescription drugs ($500). This means you will have to pay $750 ($250 + $500) of the first $2,250 of drug purchases, which may be less than you are paying currently, depending on your situation. It does not get better after that, since there is *no coverage* on the next $2,850 worth of drug expenses.

Therefore, if you participate in Medicare Part D you will be responsible for $3,600 of the first $5,100 of prescription drug expenses. Finally, after you have had $5,100 of prescription drug purchases, coverage begins again. For any prescription drug expenses after the $5,100 total, you will pay either $2 for a generic drug, $5 for a brand name drug, or 5% of the cost of the drug, *whichever is greater.*

> **Example:** *You have already paid $5,100 of pre-scription drug purchases during the year. Your next prescription is for a brand name drug that costs $200. You would be responsible for $10, which is 5% of the $200 and greater than the $5 amount set by the government.*

More generous rules apply for low-income individuals. The qualifying limits will be set in 2005.

Is Medicare Part D mandatory? The answer is no. However, if you do not elect it, your premiums for Part B of Medicare will increase about 10% in 2005 and then 5% per year after that. Furthermore, beginning in 2007, if your income is over $80,000, you will pay even more for Part B. The costs will be based on a sliding scale.

Medical Supplement Insurance (Medigap)

In addition to Medicare, many people purchase supple-mental health insurance policies, commonly referred to as Medigap policies. These policies are purchased from private insurance companies and pay for items and costs not covered by Medicare. However, they do not cover everything. Some items not covered include eye care, dental care, hearing aids, private nurses, and long-term care. Ten standardized plans, labeled A through J, are available. Each plan specifies a different level of coverage. The most basic is plan A, which will pay most hospital charge copayments and doctor's bills that Medicare will not cover. Every insurer must offer this level of coverage. Make sure the policy you purchase is "guaranteed renewable," so you cannot be refused as you grow older. If you can afford it, I believe it is wise to have a supplemental health insurance policy.

You may be worried about your health and think that you may not qualify for a health insurance policy because of a preexisting condition. *This will not be a problem if you apply within six months of enrolling in the Medicare program.* During this period, you have guaranteed access to coverage from any insurance company selling coverage in your state. There are many variations on which plans are available from state to state, so check with an advisor in your state. If you sign up and within the first 30 days decide it is not for you, the policy can be cancelled and you will receive a full refund.

Some types of supplemental health insurance policies also offer prescription drug coverage. This, however, is quite expensive to have, but many people choose this feature. The new Medicare prescription drug law will affect Medigap policies that have drug coverage. People currently enrolled in a Medigap policy *without* a drug benefit will not be affected. The Medigap plan will continue to cover Medicare's cost sharing for physician and hospital services.

People currently enrolled in a Medigap policy with drug coverage will have two choices. First, they are able to keep their Medigap plan with the drug benefit. However, they could be subject to penalty if they later decide to enroll in Medicare Part D. In addition, remember the Medicare part B premium increases for those not enrolled in Part D. Second, they can enroll in Medicare Part D, keep their current Medigap plan, but drop their Medigap plan's drug benefits and thus pay a lower premium. In the future, people will likely only be able to purchase a Medigap policy that does not have drug coverage.

Chapter Twenty-nine

Social Security

Your Social Security benefit will most likely be an important piece of your retirement plan. If you did not begin collecting your widow's Social Security benefit when your spouse passed away or you were not eligible, you will need to decide when to start collecting Social Security. You must first decide if you want to begin collecting benefits at age 62, at full retirement age, or somewhere in between. Full retirement age has changed. It used to be age 65, but now there are many ages depending on your date of birth, as shown in Table 3 on the following page.

In my opinion, except in certain situations, I advise people to begin receiving Social Security at age 62. Why? One big reason: I am concerned with the future ability of the government to continue to pay the benefit. This is no secret. Debates have been going on for years about the viability of the Social Security system. I believe the burden of keeping the program going strong into the future will be quite difficult.

Table 3. Retirement Age

Year of Birth	Full Retirement Age
1937 or earlier	65
1938	65 and 2 months
1939	65 and 4 months
1940	65 and 6 months
1941	65 and 8 months
1942	65 and 10 months
1943 – 1954	66
1955	66 and 2 months
1956	66 and 4 months
1957	66 and 6 months
1958	66 and 8 months
1959	66 and 10 months
1960 and later	67

An easy way for the government to solve this problem does exist, and I believe it will eventually be chosen as the answer. Two words describe the answer—"means testing." This could be handled in the following way. The government will develop some level of savings or net worth amount and if your assets exceed it, you will not get all of your benefit. If your assets reach a predetermined higher level, you won't receive any Social Security benefit. So, I believe it is better to start collecting early before the rules are changed. "A bird in hand is better than two in the bush." Remember, this is my *opinion* and not currently part of any proposed legislation or law. However, when we are planning, we often must look at what may likely happen, and plan for it.

When would I wait until later than age 62? In 2004, if you are under the age of 65, still working and earning more than $11,640, you will be required to pay back a portion of your Social Security benefit. For every $2 you earn over $11,640 in 2004, you are required to give $1 back to the government. The year you reach full retirement age, you are allowed to earn $31,080, and repay $1 for every $3 you earn over this amount. Therefore, if you are earning in excess of these amounts before age 65 or in the year you reach full retirement age, I would consider not taking your Social Security benefit early. If you are only slightly over the limit, such as $1,000, it may not be significant, but if you were $6,000 over, I would not elect to take Social Security early. These earnings limitations are indexed to inflation and increase each year.

If you earn more than the allowed amount in the years *after* you reach full retirement age, there are no rules requiring you to return any of your benefit. This would allow a person who needs to keep working for a living to collect their benefit in addition to their earned income. It is important to note that the government can change these rules at any time.

A major question you probably have is "What will my future Social Security benefit be?" You may already be collecting a benefit if you have retired. If this is the case, you will now have the choice of collecting the larger of your current benefit or what your deceased spouse's actual benefit was or would have been. If you have not yet reached retirement age and are not yet collecting, your benefit will be based upon the average earnings of your highest 35 earning years of your career. If you have not worked for a total of 35 years, the years you did not work will be considered as years with zero wages. Thus, your average earnings and benefit will be lower. Once again, if your deceased spouse was entitled to a larger benefit, you are entitled to receive your spouse's actual amount instead of the amount based on your working career.

To apply for your Social Security benefit, you should call the local Social Security office. To find the telephone number of your local office, look in your telephone directory under the government section. If you cannot find a local number, you can call 1-800-772-1213. You can also obtain information on the Internet. The Web site address of the Social Security Administration is www.ssa.gov. When you apply, you will need to provide certain documents, depending on your situation. The following information will be needed.

- Social Security number
- Birth certificate
- W-2 forms or self-employment tax return for last year

- Military discharge papers if you had military service

- Proof of U.S. citizenship if you were not born in the United States

- Bank account name and account number, for direct deposit

You will need to submit original documents or copies that have been certified by the issuing office. If you do not have a document, the Social Security Administration can help you obtain it.

Estate Planning for Singles

In Part I, Chapter 4, estate planning for a married couple was covered. Your estate plan as it was originally set up may still meet your needs. However, changes may be warranted in some situations. At some point you may remarry, or you may change your mind about your current estate plan and want to revise it. This section covers some of the issues that should concern you if changes need to be made.

Wills

If you have a will in place that carries out your wishes and makes sense in light of current laws, you need not change anything. However, if you do not have a will or the one you have no longer fulfills your needs, you need to take action.

The type of will needed at this point will be less complex than when you were married. In most cases, a simple will should satisfy your needs. This document will allow you to leave your assets to whom you wish and allow you to take advantage of the applicable exclusion amount, the amount that can be passed on at death without incurring estate tax. (See Chapter 4 in Part I.) The simple will states that when you pass on, your estate should distribute your assets in the manner dictated in the will. Normally, a testamentary trust (one that is set up at death) is not needed if you are not married. You may still want to use a testamentary trust, however, if the individual you are leaving assets to is not competent or capable of handling their inheritance. The trust would be set up at your death and the trustee you name would be responsible for managing the assets in the trust. Income from the trust can be distributed to the beneficiary on a regular basis as determined by the trust language.

Durable Power of Attorney and Advance Directives

If you do not have a durable power of attorney and an advance directive in place, you need to have this done. Please see the discussion regarding these in Chapter 4. In most cases your deceased spouse was your agent. You may want to consider naming one or more of your children as your agents. Remember, the person you name must be trustworthy, so give it some thought before choosing an agent. It is important to have these documents prepared if you do not have them, or revised if needed, if you do have them.

Living Trusts

Because of the changes that have taken place in your life, this may be the appropriate time to consider having a revocable living trust created, if you currently do not have one. Please see Chapter 4 for an in-depth discussion of revocable living trusts.

Before the death of your spouse, depending on your situation, probate may have been avoided by having assets titled properly. This is more difficult, now that you are alone. This can be done by owning your assets jointly with your children, which I would not advise. If you own assets jointly with your children and they get themselves in financial trouble, the joint accounts are available for creditors to satisfy their claims. Another alternative as discussed in the "Avoiding Probate" section of Chapter 4 would be to title your bank accounts and investment accounts payable on death (POD) and transfer on death (TOD).

But even if you do this, real estate is going to be difficult to keep out of probate. Some techniques may protect your house from probate, but in one form or another, you are giving your house away and that may not fit your needs. These techniques are beyond the scope of this book. So even though your current will may still be appropriate, it will most likely not keep your estate out of probate. If this is a concern for you, consider using a revocable living trust as your main estate-planning tool. The cost to create the trust could be $1,500 to $2,000, but probate could cost $5,000 to $10,000. It is a "pay now" or "pay later" situation.

Gifting

A simple technique used by many who are facing an eventual estate tax problem is gifting. You are allowed to make a gift to anyone you wish, and it is not limited to one person. You can gift to as many people as you desire. The most important rule to understand is that the *amount of the gift is limited.* 2004 rules allow you to gift $11,000 to each individual you choose. This is known as the annual exclusion amount and is indexed for inflation. The amount will change again when cost of living adjustments reach the next $1,000 multiple. At that time, the amount will change to $12,000. Another rule is that the gift must be of a present interest, meaning the recipient must enjoy all rights of ownership such as use, enjoyment, possession and income. Most gifts to a trust do not qualify because generally the rights of ownership come later.

If you want to gift more than $11,000 to someone, you have to file a gift tax return and may have to pay a gift tax on the amount gifted that is over $11,000. Each individual is allowed to gift up to $1,000,000 total in their lifetime without having to pay a gift tax. Each dollar that you use of the $1,000,000 by gifting also reduces the applicable exclusion amount available to reduce your taxable estate. There can be benefits to using the $1,000,000 gift exclusion during your life. When you make a gift during your lifetime, any future growth on the property gifted is no longer part of your estate.

> *Example: John Doe gifts $1,000,000 of stock to his children today. There is no tax on the gift when it is made due to the $1,000,000 lifetime gift exclusion. When John Doe passes away, his applicable exclusion amount will be reduced by $1,000,000. If John lives 20 more years after making the gift and in that time the gifted property grows to a value of $3,000,000, John will have removed the $2,000,000 of growth on the gifted property from his estate.*

The $11,000 annual gift exclusion is not considered part of the $1,000,000 amount. This means that you could gift $1,011,000 in one year without incurring a gift tax. Any year after that, you would be limited to the $11,000 annual exclusion.

However, there is an exception to the $11,000 exclusion limit. You are allowed to pay tuition and medical expenses for an individual without limitation. As long as these payments are made directly to the school or medical provider, they are not considered part of your annual or lifetime exclusions. Payments for books, supplies, and room and board *do not* qualify. Tuition for part-time students does qualify. Any medical expenses that would be deductible on your federal income tax return, including insurance premiums, qualify. You would not be allowed a tax deduction for the medical expense unless the benefiting individual is your dependent.

Chapter Thirty-one

Education Funding

If you would like to help your grandchildren with their college costs, consider using a Section 529 plan. A Section 529 College Savings plan is becoming the most popular vehicle for funding education costs. Each state has a plan. You can use any plan you would like, but some states offer tax incentives for using your home-state plan. These normally have income limitations and it may not benefit you depending on your level of income. Nonetheless, you should still give your home-state plan a look.

These plans offer many benefits. First, the earnings from plan investments will be tax free if the money withdrawn from the plan is used to pay qualified education costs. Qualified expenses under a 529 plan represent a wider range of expenses than the gifting rules discussed in Chapter 30. In addition to tuition, other qualified expenses are room and board, books, and other supplies. Also, you maintain control of the account over time. With traditional education funding vehicles, such as trusts and UGMA (Uniform Gift to Minors Act) accounts, the beneficiaries can access the account upon reaching the age of adulthood. When the child goes to postsecondary school, you direct payments from the account. If the beneficiary does not go to school, you can change the beneficiary. If you have no further beneficiaries to designate, you can make yourself the beneficiary or withdraw the funds. Beware: If you withdraw the funds for a nonqualified purpose, you will be subject to a 10% penalty plus income taxes on any earnings that have built up in the account.

Generally, you can only gift $11,000 per year per individual, as discussed earlier. However, with a 529 plan you can make five years' worth of gifts in one year. You can contribute up to $55,000 per beneficiary into a 529 plan for as many beneficiaries as you would like. However, once you do this you cannot make any more gifts to these individuals for any purpose over the next five years because you have used up the five annual exemption amounts (5 x $11,000). There can be only one beneficiary for each 529 plan you set up. If you want to contribute to a 529 plan for more than one individual, you will need to set up separate accounts for each person. Units of a 529 plan investment option are municipal securities and may be subject to market value fluctuations.

Second Marriages

It may not seem possible to you right now, but you could remarry. I always say, "Never say never." Life is full of too many surprises to rule out anything. It is impossible to see down the road and know what twists and turns our lives may take. I have seen two people come together in a second marriage many times—it is wonderful to see people who had been lonely find happiness again. If you do remarry, a couple of issues should be considered: prenuptial agreements and qualified terminal interest property (QTIP) trusts.

The first time you marry an attitude of "What's mine is yours and what's yours is mine" usually prevails. In a second marriage this is much less likely to be the case and is especially true when either of the couple has children from a first marriage. The above-mentioned agreement and trust are important tools to protect assets in a second marriage.

Prenuptial Agreements

A prenuptial agreement is a binding agreement entered into before marriage in which the parties set forth what will happen in the event the marriage ends, either by divorce or because of death. Creating a prenuptial agreement can cause strain on the relationship at the worst possible time. No one marries with the expectation that it will end in divorce, but that does not mean we should not plan for it. Let's face it, the reality is that more people are divorcing today than ever before.

In addition, this agreement dictates what will happen if either spouse dies, so you are planning for more than just divorce. Your future spouse's will can't supersede the prenuptial agreement if the will is less generous. But a will can be more generous than the prenuptial agreement and leave you more than what was stated in the agreement. No matter how you feel right now, it may be prudent to implement a prenuptial agreement. Is it for everyone? No, but most people should at least consider one. The list that follows offers some decision guidelines. Consider a prenuptial agreement if:

- You own assets, such as a home, stock, or retirement funds.

- You own all or part of a business.

- You anticipate receiving an inheritance.

- You have children and/or grandchildren from a previous marriage.

- One spouse is much wealthier than the other.

- One spouse will be supporting the other through college.

- You have loved ones who need to be taken care of, such as elderly parents.

- You have or are pursuing a degree or license in a potentially lucrative profession, such as medicine, or are starting a successful business.

If you decide on a prenuptial agreement, have an attorney draft the agreement for you. However, before you see the attorney, discuss this with your partner and come to an understanding about key elements in the agreement and how you believe it should operate. When having this discussion, it is vital that both individuals are honest and disclose all that they own. Having this discussion before seeing the attorney should save you money and not waste the attorney's time.

The fees for such an agreement will most likely be related to the amount of time the attorney spends drafting the agreement. With attorneys charging $200 or more per hour you can see why it would be advantageous to reduce their time as much as possible. Both spouses should hire their own attorneys. This will help show that both parties had legal representation and help ensure the agreement is enforceable. The agreement should be signed well in advance of the wedding—at least 30 days before would be a good idea. This will help avoid the appearance of coercion.

The agreement also must be fair to both spouses. It cannot have the effect of leaving one spouse destitute.

The agreement should deal with any of the issues on the above list that are relevant, as well as future income, new asset purchases, etc. Each specific topic should be addressed, determining who receives which property or has a right to future cash flows if the marriage ends. Without this type of agreement, your assets may end up with someone you do not want to have them.

Qualified Terminal Interest Property (QTIP) Trusts

If you have children from a prior marriage and remarry, you will probably be concerned that the children from your first marriage inherit the property you and your deceased spouse accumulated over the years you were together. In most cases, the person you are marrying may have the same situation and feel the same way. This issue can be handled in a couple of different ways. You could just leave your assets outright to your children when you die. Or you may want your surviving spouse to have income from your assets while they are still alive and after their death pass the asset on to your heirs. A QTIP trust is designed to handle the second concern. The QTIP trust guarantees that the decedent's assets ultimately end up in the hands of their children or other designated heirs.

The QTIP trust allows the first spouse to die to give lifetime benefits (like income earned on the trust assets) to their spouse while restricting the spouse's access to the principal. The surviving spouse, however, can use the principal if necessary (at the discretion of the trustee of the QTIP), for their health, education, support, and maintenance. When the surviving spouse dies, the trust then pays the remaining assets to your children or designated heirs. *As with all legal documents, seek a qualified attorney to prepare them for you.*

Many other complicated estate planning techniques are available, but they are beyond the scope of this book. If you have advanced problems, an estate planning attorney should be able to assist you.

Conclusion

Losing a spouse and being on your own will result in some of the most challenging times of your life. However, proper planning should make it just a little easier to face those difficult times.

The best time to plan is *before* someone passes away. By being organized and laying out a road map in advance, the surviving spouse should have an easier and better path to follow while grieving and rebuilding their life. And remember, do not underestimate the power of optimism and a good sense of humor.

If you purchased or received this book after your spouse's death, it is not too late to make things easier on yourself or your heirs by following the suggestions I have laid out. As mentioned throughout the book, if you do not have the expertise, hire a professional. The time lost and potential problems you will avoid makes it a smart move on your part. And, it is usually easier to get things accomplished when you work as part of a team—or maybe even just thinking there is a team—like our friend Trigger in this, our final humorous tale...

A person from the big city was driving his car in the country when he went into the ditch. Just by luck, a farmer happened to be coming down the road walking a big strong horse. The city fellow asked the farmer if he would give him a hand. The farmer said he would and proceeded to tie a rope to the horse and to the frame of the car. Then the farmer hollered "Pull, Junior, Pull." Trigger stood still. Next, the farmer yelled "Pull, Pepper, Pull" and again Trigger did not move. Then the farmer commanded, "Pull, Ginger, Pull," and Trigger did not budge. Finally the farmer screamed, "Pull, Trigger, Pull," and Trigger dragged the car right out of the ditch. The city fellow was thankful and very impressed. He then asked the farmer why he yelled four different names when trying to get the horse to pull. The farmer said, "You see, Trigger is blind, and if he thought he was the only one pulling, he wouldn't even try."

Index